MURDER

Anarchy or Ethical Behavior in the Twenty-First Century

Charles G. Wright, Jr.

WALDENHOUSE PUBLISHERS, INC.
WALDEN, TENNESSEE

MURDER: Anarchy or Ethical Behavior in the Twenty-First Century

Published by Waldenhouse Publishers, Inc.
100 Clegg Street, Signal Mountain, Tennessee 37377 USA
423-886-2721 www.waldenhouse.com
Type and Design by Karen Paul Stone
Printed in the United States of America
ISBN: 978-1-947589-52-0
Library of Congress Control Number: 2022944091

A criticism of the human tendency to demand non violence within nations but to praise and reward it when making war with other nations. Demonstrates the wisdom and feasibility of making war illegal under present circumstances. - provided by Publisher

Law 026000 Criminal Law/General
Law 051000 International
Law 109000 Governmental/General

Dedication

This book is dedicated to all those being killed in war because the peaceful do nothing to prevent it.

Table of Contents

Chapter 1

"There is no salvation for civilization or even the human race, other than the creation of a world government."
- Albert Einstein

"It is my conviction that killing under the cloak of war is nothing but an act of murder." - Albert Einstein

Having a world government is an alien concept to most people. The human race accepts implicitly the idea that international war is inevitable. We do not tend to think about the idea of having a world government. This book has as its purpose proposing a limited world government to stop humans from killing each other.

No country in the world does not seriously punish the killing of another human being in its country by a private person. However, each country in the world honors its war heroes for killing enemies of the nation. Some high military decorations in a few representative nations are as follows:

1. United Kingdom – The Victoria Cross
2. Thailand – Order of Roma
3. Bulgaria – Order of Bravery
4. Estonia – The Cross of Liberty
5. Austria – The Military Merit Decoration

6. Greece – Medal for Gallantry
7. Israel – Medal of Valor
8. United States – Medal of Honor
9. Zimbabwe – Gold Cross of Zimbabwe
10. Argentina – Cross to the Heroic Valor in combat
11. Brazil – Order of Military Merit
12. Colombia – Order of San Mateo
13. Italy – Gold Medal of Military Valor
14. India – Param Vis Chakra
15. France – The Legion of Honour
16. Germany – The Cross of Honour for Valor
17. Portugal – Order of the Tower and Sword

The nations of the world clearly see nothing morally wrong with killing human beings as long as they are the ones doing the killing. However, if you do the killing and not the government, you are certainly going to lose your freedom or your life. In other words, sovereign states engage in situational ethics in its most corrupted form.

Throughout human history, each level of human organization had to do and did do something about dealing with murder within the group. Over time humans have organized themselves in progressively larger groups and each larger group dealt with the murder of another human being within the group by punishments that reasonably controlled that type of behavior. The world's problem with war is that it has not yet established the organizational structure to control organized murder at the world level.

Governments proscribe killing because to do otherwise would destroy the governmental unit from within. War at the world level is a danger to the world just like one person killing his neighbor is a danger to a tribe.

Those who oppose a world government that can put an end to war would, with the same logic, support doing away with punishment for murder within nations. If that were done, the whole human race would implode.

Moses is said to have come off Mount Sinai with the 10 Commandments from God which included the command to not murder. This took place around 1446 BC. The Jewish people then proceeded to conquer Jericho and Ai, conquer the southern cities in Canaan and defeat King Jabin of Hazor. This is just one of the many, many examples of your morals only applying to your people but not outsiders. Humans switch their moral thinking like this example all the time and have been doing it for hundreds of thousands of years. This contradiction is built in our genes and will continue to haunt the human race until our governmental structure is set up in a manner that will stop it from expressing itself in a negative way.

Every person in every country of the world finds themselves in an ethical contradiction. On the one hand they are saying to the world that in my country it is wrong to kill other persons. In fact, my country has severe penalties for doing this. The judicial system in my country is set up to prosecute and punish persons who kill other people. Killing is wrong and my country does something about it if it takes place.

On the other hand, every person in the world is saying to every person in other countries that it is not wrong to kill them if my country so chooses. Killing them is not wrong and I can kill people in other countries whenever my country wants to. When I kill people in other countries, I will not and should not be punished because it is not wrong to kill people in other countries in war. People's lives in countries other than mine are not as important as lives in my country. I have no ethical obligation toward them. I should be able to continue to kill them anytime my country wants.

It is not hard to figure out why humans can simultaneously believe killing a person in their own culture is the worst of all behaviors and believing killing in war is worthy of the highest honors. The contradiction demonstrates how malleable cultural values can be. Usually, cultural values can vary radically between cultures but in the present context, the values are the same in almost every culture but the contradiction between the two values involved couldn't be more extreme and presently irrational.

Our values are determined by our superego which is a part of our psyche which imposes not only values for what we should do but also feelings of conscience for what we should not do. The superego is developed during our childhood by influence from our parents and our culture. In other words, we internalize what we are taught by our parents and culture. The fact that mandates by the superego are contradictory is seldom thought about by the conscious mind.

These contradictory values of the superego were developed over hundreds of thousands of years and assured that those who believed the contradictory values were better able to survive. The contradictory nature of these values does not aid survival today but greatly impairs our survival as a species.

Unless we teach our children to internalize a moral value of world peace, we are doomed. Our children need to be taught to aspire for attaining peace and to feel pangs of conscience in making war. Our children's superego needs to be reprogrammed for survival in the modern world conditions.

Chapter 2

"War can only be abolished by the establishment of a world government." – Bertrand Russell

"War does not determine who is right, only who is left." – Bertrand Russell

The League of Nations was formed on June 28, 1919, as part of the Treaty of Versailles which ended World War One. The covenant of the League of Nations became effective on January 10, 1920. The League of Nations lasted until April 20, 1946. The League of Nations was formed to encourage peace and prevent another world war. It did not prevent World War Two.

The League of Nations Assembly consisted of representatives from all member nations. Each member nation got one vote. The League also had a Council and a permanent secretariat. A unanimous vote based upon national sovereignty of member nations, was required for all decisions of the Assembly and Council with only minor exceptions.

The Council had initially four permanent members: 1) United Kingdom, 2) France, 3) Italy, and 4) Japan. In the negotiations over the language of the Covenant, France had wanted to form an international army to enforce the League's decisions. However, other nations objected and an international army never became a reality. Had such an army become reality, the League of Nations may still be in existence today.

The General Assembly met once a year and consisted of representatives of all member states. It decided on the organization's policies.

The Assembly could only make a decision by unanimous vote so it never made any decisions.

On the Council all the permanent members had a vote.

The Conference of Ambassadors kept overruling decisions of the Council.

Germany joined the League in 1926 and left in 1935. In September 1934, the Soviet Union entered the League of Nations, but was expelled in 1939 for invading Finland. At its largest, The League consisted of 58 member nations.

The League was also useless in reacting to German remilitarization which was a violation of the Treaty of Versailles.

Germany and Japan voluntarily withdrew in 1933 – Italy left in 1937.

The United States never joined despite the fact that the League was the brain child of President Woodrow Wilson.

In 1927, the foreign affairs minister for France, Aristide Briand, proposed an agreement with the United States of America that war would be outlawed between the two nations. The United States feared that such an agreement might be interpreted so as to require the United States to come to France's defense if France was attacked. However, United States' Secretary of State, Frank B. Kellogg, proposed other nations could join the agreement which would outlaw wars of aggression but not military acts of self-defense. Fifteen nations signed the agreement at first and later another forty-seven nations signed. Because there was no way to enforce violations of the agreement, the agreement became useless after multiple violations by signing countries. The agreement was called the Kellogg-Briand Pact, 1928.

When the United Nations was started in 1945 there were 50 nations which were members. At the present time, there are 193 nations who are member nations of the United Nations. The United Nations, as its charter exists today, is committed to honoring the sovereignty of its 193 nations who can go to war anytime they please and for whatever reason they choose. In other words, each nation has 192 other nations it potentially could go to war with without getting permission from anyone and without punishment of any nation. There are 37,056 possible combinations for how this could happen.

It is no exaggeration to say that every nation that is a member of the United Nations was formed directly or indirectly by war. In most all instances the history of the territory of the present nations has seen multiple wars that have ultimately resulted in the present nation. The second world war was instrumental in the formation of the United Nations. Five permanent members of the Security Council were the victors in the Second World War. The losers in that war (Italy, Germany, and Japan) were not made permanent members of the Security Council.

Two world wars taught us that we had to do something for world peace. Albert Einstein is quoted as saying, "I know not with what weapons World War III will be fought, but World War IV will be fought with sticks and stones."

Since the formation of the United Nations in 1945, we have proven that the world's nations can sit down and discuss problems in a peaceful manner. The United Nations has limited powers and is subject to a veto power by any permanent member of the Security Council. The same permanent members can also veto amendments to the charter.

The United Nations needs to evolve in the direction of having more power for all nations of the world.

The United Nations' Security Council has the duty of trying to maintain peace in the world. It has five permanent members: China, France, Russian Federation, United Kingdom and United States. It also has ten non-permanent members who are elected to two-year terms by the General Assembly of the United Nations. More than 50 members of the United Nations have never been elected to the Security Council.

The General Assembly of the United Nations is composed of all 193 member nations. It has a limited role in maintaining peace but a key role in financing peace operations.

The five-country veto on the Security Council is another way of saying that the United Nations is a dictatorship. In fact, it has five dictators instead of one. Besides the Security Council simply voting not to take action in any one situation, the veto power of the five permanent members means there are five other ways to take no action to stop a war. The Security Council, therefore, is simply dysfunctional as well as unfair to the other countries in the world.

In 1948, three years after the beginning of the United Nations, the General Assembly of the United Nations adopted the Universal Declaration of Human Rights. This consisted of a preamble and 30 articles which stated what were believed to be the rights to which every human was entitled.

The minute the Universal Declaration of Human Rights was adopted, the structure of the United Nations prevented it living up to the following:

1) The preamble stated "that human rights should be protected by the rule of law." The failure of the United Nations to have enforceable laws against war has been the direct cause of hundreds of thousands of deaths in war. The preamble also states: "whereas it is essential to promote the development of friendly relations between nations." The lack of enforceable dispute resolution laws has been the direct cause of hundreds of thousands of deaths in war.

2) Article 3 states: "Everyone has the right to life, liberty and security of person." The right to life could be protected better by enforceable laws against murder by nations.

3) Article 5 states: "No one shall be subjected to torture or cruel, inhumane or degrading treatment or punishment." Every war that the United Nations allows violates this article.

4) Article 6 states: "Everyone has the right to recognition everywhere as a person before the law" Allowing sovereign nations to be above enforceable laws violates this article.

5) Article 7 reads: "all are equal before the law and are entitled without any discrimination to equal protection of the law. All are entitled to equal protection against any discrimination in violation of this declaration and against any incitement to such discrimination." Without enforceable laws against member nations, the United Nations cannot equally protect anyone.

6) Article 28 reads: "Everyone is entitled to a social and international order in which the rights and freedoms set forth in this declaration can be fully realized." The United Nations has failed to establish an international order to assure that the Universal Declaration of Human Rights become a reality.

The international community is to be commended for adopting the Universal Declaration of Human Rights. But the reality of the present state of the world is that by not outlawing war, the countries of the world are saying they have defacto a right to kill thousands of persons in other countries anytime they wish, with impunity. Where is the Human Rights Code that protects us from this inhumanity?

In one sense, it is hard to imagine a more inconsistent organization than the United Nations. The Executive Office of the Secretary General of the United Nations has a Rule of Law Unit located at the United Nations' Headquarters, First Avenue at 46th Street, New York, New York. This unit has a website that tells of the many advantages and virtues of the Rule of Law. Of course, this only applies to the rule of law at the national and lower level of government. It does not apply at the international level because the 193 nations of the United Nations have anointed themselves with sovereignty by the charter of the United Nations. This means they have supreme authority over their nation and are not subject to the international restraint of law. This is the best of all possible worlds for 193 nations. They cajole their citizens by means of the Rule of Law Unit to obey the law within their nations while declaring themselves above the law. In other words, they punish persons for murder under their own laws but engage in mass murder through wars with impunity. The 193 nations of the world are therefore omnipotent and inhabit the same small planet which consists of only 30% dry land. People despair of ever finding a solution to the problem of war. The solution lies in not giving omnipotence to 193 nations.

Individuals are not omnipotent. Villages are not omnipotent. Cities are not omnipotent. States within a nation are not omnipotent. Why should nations be omnipotent? There are no logical reasons why they should be considered sovereign, and therefore, omnipotent on the international stage. If they were not considered sovereign and were subject to an international law against war, most of the murders in the world would not take place.

The net effect of the statements in the preceding paragraphs is that the 193 nations in the United Nations expect the world to obey their laws in the future, but they expect they will maintain their omnipotence in the future. This is an ominous sign for world peace in the future of the human race.

Article 108 of Chapter XVIII of the United Nations' Charter reads as follows:

Article 108:

"Amendments to the present Charter shall come into force for all members of the United Nations when they have been adopted by a vote of two thirds of the General Assembly and ratified in accordance with their respective constitutional processes by two thirds of the members of the United Nations, including all permanent members of the Security Council."

The Charter has been amended five times.

1. In 1965, Article 23 was amended to enlarge the Security Council from 11 to 15 members;

2. In 1965, Article 27 was amended to increase the required number of Security Council votes from 7 to 9;

3. In 1965, Article 61 was amended to enlarge the Economic and Social Council from 18 to 27 members;

4. In 1968, Article 109 was amended to change the requirements for a General Conference of Member States for reviewing the Charter;

5. In 1973, Article 61 was again amended to further enlarge the Economic and Social Council from 27 to 54 members.

The name United Nations is a misnomer. The 193 nations that are members have never been united, are not united now and will not be in the future as long as sovereignty is recognized. The governmental subdivisions of the United Kingdom, United States and United Arab Emirates do not have the legal right to make war among themselves. This is not the case with the United Nations. Any country in the United Nations can engage in war with any other country and pay no price for killing people in the process. Member nations spend huge amounts of money and time in building up their militaries to potentially fight other members they are supposedly united with. They do not trust each other. The United Nations is about as united as a human body that is overwhelmed with metastatic cancer. "A house divided against itself cannot stand." – Mark 3:25

There is no place in the United Nations' Charter where it says that the United Nations was organized to have a limited existence in time. Presumably, it will be in existence as long as it can maintain its existence. We do know that the Charter says that Great Britain, the United States, China, Russia, and France are permanent members of the Security Council and they each can exercise a veto over resolutions of the Security Council and any proposed amendments to the Charter. Permanent is a word that has a very clear and unmistakable meaning. Each of the permanent members has a vested interest in not giving up their veto power. While it may sound like common sense, much research has been done to prove that persons with vested interests are slow to agree to measures that will affect their privilege.

Since 1945, the five permanent members of the Security Council of the UN have maintained their veto power of any peace keeping by the UN. They have maintained their veto power over any changes to the Charter for the same length of time. Over the same length of time, they have been successful in preventing most other countries from obtaining nuclear weapons, all the while retaining such weapons. These countries are in complete control of whether there is an international effort to prevent war.

From October 1, 1990 to July 18, 1994, the Republic of Rwanda was involved in a civil war in which UN permanent member of the Security Council, France, was involved. The United Nations sent a peacekeeping force but its Charter Chapter VI mandate prevented military intervention to prevent the genocide that took place in Rwanda. Approximately three quarters of a million Tutsi and moderate Hutu persons were killed in Rwandan genocide without any prevention by the United Nations.

The permanent member veto makes it impossible for the UN to act when one of the permanent members of the Security Council is involved in a war. The United States was free to conduct the Vietnam War, the war against Iraq, the war against Afghanistan, and the Korean war. It fought China in Operation Beleaguer. The US took part in the Laotian Civil War, and the Lebanon Crisis. It was involved in the Bay of Pigs Invasion, and in the First Taiwan Straights Crisis. It took part in the Simba Rebellion in the Congo. The U.S. took part in the Communist Insurgency in Thailand, and in the Dominican Republic Civil War. The United States took part in the insurgency in Bolivia, the Cambodian Civil War, the war in South Zaire, Gulf of Sadia encounter, multination intervention in Lebanon, Grenada, bombing of Libya, the Tanker War, Tobruk Encounter, Invasion of Panama, Gulf War, Somali Civil War, Bosnian War, Haiti, Kosovo, Operation Ocean Shield, Yemen, and fought in the Jinjiang Conflict.

Without listing all the wars of France, Russia and the United Kingdom since 1945, it is clear that the United Nations does nothing to stop wars by permanent members of the Security Council, with veto power.

If being victors in the Second World War justified the five permanent members of the United Nations in having a veto power in the United Nations' Security Counsel, why not give more power to the winners of other wars? Spain conquered most of South and Central America, so why not give them a permanent seat at the table. Alexander the Great, from Macedonia, conquered most all of the known world. Mongolia conquered just about everybody they attacked. The Vikings in Scandinavia were pretty successful in overwhelming Europe. Rome, in Italy, defeated just about everyone in sight to establish their empire. The reason none of these victors merit a permanent United Nations veto is because their military victories do not justify giving them power over everybody else and that's the same reason the present permanent members have no defensible reason for having power over everybody else. As the philosophers of the enlightenment have suggested, people should be governed by their consent. Might does not make right.

How much longer are the victors of the Second World War supposed to keep the veto power over the rest of the world? That concept could go on for centuries or longer. In small primitive groups abuse of others within the group is put up with until the people finally take the law into their own hands and kill the repeat offender. Power obtained through force is likely to be overthrown by force. The proper remedy is to be fair to begin with.

The Second World War was undoubtedly a tremendous tragedy for the world, but it was only one period in history. The formation of the United Nations was a direct result of being successful in the Second World War. The veto power of the victors was obviously for the purpose of keeping the victors in control after the defeat of their enemies. It has little relevance today. Japan, Germany and Italy have not been at war with anyone since 1945. There is no reason for the permanent members of the UN to have veto power over anything based upon what happened in the first half of the 1940s.

If we wanted to go back in history and hold grudges, France and England fought each other in the Normandy Invasion and in the hundred years war.

The United States and the Soviet Union were involved in the cold war. France, under Napoleon, fought Russia. Great Britain fought the opium war with China. The United States fought for its independence from Great Britain and fought the war of 1812 with Great Britain. One could logically claim that the victors of the Second World War should have never been allies to begin with, because once you have fought someone, you can never trust them again.

It is an actuarial probability that there are no or very few combatants from the Second World War even alive today. What are the permanent members of the Security Council of the United Nations protecting themselves from by maintaining their veto power?

There is a basic principle of good management that says responsibility and authority should match one another. If someone has authority over a certain activity, they are responsible for the results from that activity. If someone is held responsible for the results, then they have to have the authority to affect the outcome.

In light of this principle, who is responsible for world anarchy and wars since 1945? The answer is clear. The countries that are responsible are the winners of the Second World War who set up the United Nations and gave themselves veto power over any kind of peace making through the Security Council. 1) Great Britain, 2) United States, 3) Russia, 4) France, and 5) China. They also each have a veto power over any amendments to the United States Charter. Other countries do not have a veto power over anything in the United Nations and have only a small chance of serving on the Security Council for limited periods. The United Nations is really not designed for peace. It is designed to allow the victors in a world war to be in control of the world. The way they have designed the power structure of the world, it is absolutely certain that sovereign nations will continue to make war and kill each other. Blame the permanent members of the Security Council. They designed the system which they protect from amendment of the Charter with their veto. A system set up from being victors in a world war is not legitimate. It just is. The rest of the countries in the world are very similar to defeated persons sent to Rome to be slaves in the imperial Roman Empire. They are subject to the power of the conquerors.

The United Nations espouses certain characteristics that constitute good governance. The problem is that neither the United Nations or any other entity at the world level follows any of the suggested characteristics. The United Nations participates in world anarchy and preaches to nations how to govern. The characteristics that are not followed by the world's international level are:

1. Participation
2. Rule of Law
3. Transparency
4. Responsiveness
5. Equity
6. Effectiveness and efficiency
7. Consensus orientation

Mediation is the process in which a mediator is a neutral third party that attempts to get the parties to settle their disagreement where there is a real government and not a dysfunctional group of "sovereign states." If the parties cannot reach an agreement, the matter is moved along in the adjudication process for determination by a court, and possible appeals from there.

Mediation does not work in every case. In fact, it often does not work and the court has to make a determination according to law. Theoretically, the mediating parties rationally assess their chances of success in Court and come to a decision based upon the certainty or uncertainty of success in Court. All it takes is one of the two parties to misjudge their chances of success in Court and then no agreement is reached. Rationality is a trait of the human race but it does not mean that everyone does it well. Human brains have plenty of areas that do not deal with reason. Freudian psychology tells us a lot of our motivation is unconscious.

The United Nations commonly mediates disputes in international and intranational disputes, but if an agreement is not reached, there is no adjudicative process for putting an end to the matter. The parties then have the choice of doing nothing about the dispute or going to war. In far too many cases, war is the option taken. The parties then kill each other. The country with the strongest military wins and learns to fight another time when they don't like what another party is doing. The lesson is that talk doesn't solve their problems; murder does. Might seems to make right, so all the world observes this fact. Up go the military expenditures in each nation so each nation can aspire to be the toughest guy on the block. The amount spent on a bloated military takes away from worthy human objectives such as justice, ending of hunger, poverty, education, health, and solving global warming.

Lawyers within nations could never function properly if they had to depend entirely on the voluntary agreement of parties to a dispute. Disagreement between people is common even after negotiations between parties. When parties negotiate, each party estimates what would happen under the law in court. If there is no law and no court to enforce the law, there is no incentive for the parties to agree to anything. If there is law and a court, the parties have a firm basis for making a rational settlement. Of course, if the parties misjudge the strength of their cases under the law, they still could disagree. The court then decides the case. One of the main functions of having laws is to have certainty about your rights. The main function of a court is to decide the case, enforce it and put an end to the dispute. In the present anarchy at the international level, any nation can be just as unreasonable as it wants because there are no laws saying what should be done and no courts ordering that it be done.

Chapter 3

"One day, the people of the world will want peace so much that the governments are going to have to get out of their way and let them have it." – Dwight D. Eisenhower

"Every gun that is made, every warship launched, every rocket fired signifies in the final sense, a theft from those who hunger and are not fed, those who are cold and are not clothed." – Dwight D. Eisenhower

The sovereignty of a nation is the absolute right and power of an independent state to govern its affairs without any outside interference. One of the founding tenets of the United Nations was that it would not interfere in the sovereignty of the member nations.

Chapter 1, Article 2(1) of the Charter of the United Nations reads as follows:

"1. The organization is based on the principle of the sovereign equality of all its members."

Sovereignty is a modern political concept that came into being around the time of the Peace of Westphalia in 1648. This peace treaty took place in Germany and put an end to the Thirty Years War which killed approximately eight million people in many countries and the 80-year war between Spain and the Netherlands. Sovereignty meant inviolability of borders and non-interference in the domestic affairs of "sovereign" states.

The concept of sovereignty was invented to get the participants in the 30-year war and the 80-year war to resolve their differences with an agreement. Since 1648, this concept has been a basic premise of international relations up until the present. Unfortunately, it has many problems with applying it to the world in the 21st century.

In 1648 the only way to get from one nation state to another was by foot, horseback or by wind-blown ship. The world population today is approximately eighteen times what it was in 1648.

One of the reasons people are so complacent to continue to allow the wars between nations is called the social psychological concept of the Just World Phenomenon. That is, people live their lives on the assumption that the world is just and that people get what they deserve. People have a need to believe that the world is fair. If they believe the world is unfair, there would be a disturbing lack of motivation to meet daily problems. Thoughts of an unjust world are often repressed and erased from conscious memory. Mentally processing an unjust world is much more traumatic than a natural disaster because we are social animals and have a fundamental need to believe our social interaction is fair.

In other words, people generally believe the good are rewarded and the bad are punished. Psychological experiments have reported that persons who get punished are thought less of than before the punishment.

We teach our children that the good are rewarded and the bad are punished. Therefore, we are taught that we live in a just world. The reality is that we are teaching our children a lie if it is inferred that the world is just. The outcome of wars is not determined on the basis of who are good but on who kills more of their enemy. The world is unjust. Because we are taught differently as children, we live our lives based upon the Just World Phenomenon.

Today humans have plenty of means of learning about other human cultures. When we developed the distrust of other cultures, hundreds of thousands of years ago, we had absolutely no means of learning about our culture's history other than word of mouth. A children's game demonstrates how unreliable word of mouth is. Children seat themselves in a reasonably large circle and face each other toward the center of the circle. One child whispers a few words to the child next to him or her. The whispering of the same words goes around the circle and by the time it gets back to its starting point, what is being whispered is unrecognizable. Word of mouth could only be relied on for a very few repetitions. Added to this unreliability was the fact that long ago there were very small populations and very little exposure to other cultures in order to make one practiced at adjusting to other cultures. The only culture they were familiar with was what their parents indoctrinated them with. That lack of knowledge does not exist today. Ignorance of one's cultural history and other cultures is no excuse in today's world. There are many means today of having the feeling that you are a citizen of the world. Knowledge of the world is a moral responsibility. Xenophobia should be an anachronism. We should not design our political institutions for the willfully ignorant. People get as much justice as they demand through being educated.

If present day people were as ignorant and undemanding as people were a thousand or more years ago, political leaders could do practically anything they want to do, including fighting wars.

The frontal lobe of the human brain is the part of the brain which is involved in moral judgment among other higher mental functions. It is the part of our brain which evolved more recently than other parts of the brain. Our tradition of making war appears to have gone on for hundreds of thousands of years. Therefore, it seems reasonable to assume that we have inherited a custom of war which got its start when our moral sense was not as well developed as it could be today. Our distant ancestors may have not had the mental tools for dealing well with moral issues. We do not have that excuse today.

The only reason the human race has survived thus far with its warlike ways is the low human population in the past, the primitive weapons in the past, the large size of the world relative to population and difficulty of transportation around the globe.

War has the same underlying problem as global warming. Global warming has dug a hole for the human race because of rampant, parochial selfishness, without significant consideration for the whole human species.

Throughout the history of the world species have regularly become extinct. This is even worse today. The Millennium Ecosystem Assessment, developed by more than 1,000 experts, has indicated we are losing 8,700 species per year or 24 per day, because of human actions.

Persons who support the right to make war would find it difficult to point to an animal that has parts of its body attacking other parts of its body, yet that is what is recommended for homo sapiens, at the species level.

The human race today is as interconnected as the organs of the human body. Fortunately, nature has seen to it that the healthy human body works together for the benefit of all the organs. One organ does not destroy the other organs. Modern humans have not seen fit to make the world work together as efficiently as the human body. Despite the fact that the nations of the world are extremely interconnected economically and culturally, if one nation has a disagreement with another nation, the mode of dealing with the disagreement is one nation attempting to kill the other nation.

Nature has done a superb job of making the human body protect its existence. However, humans have done a very poor job of protecting themselves from each other in this highly interconnected human world. There is only one homo sapiens species, which appears to prefer the destruction of itself to protecting its existence.

There are 195 nations in the world and only 78 organs in the human body. Nations kill each other in war because the nations of the world are interacting without a brain and central nervous system, to make the human world act as one. If the human body had no brain and central nervous system body, it would be in a cemetery. Unfortunately, that is where we are all headed under present conditions.

In the last few decades psychiatrists have begun to scientifically study human happiness in earnest. Before then psychology spent most of its effort on studying mental problems as opposed to positive mental health. Great scientific studies have been made in understanding how to be happy. If our progenitors had understood what we know now about human happiness, millions of lives would have been saved from the ignorant attempts to be happy by engaging in violence and war in the past.

Psychologists have come to understand what they call the "feel-good, do-good phenomenon." Scientific studies have repeatedly proven that happiness not only makes us feel good, but it makes us more inclined to do good. Doing good does not include killing people in war.

Chapter 4

"Ours is a world of nuclear giants and ethical infants. We know more about war than we know about peace, more about killing than we know about living."
– General Omar N. Bradley

"The United Nations represents not a final stage in the development of world order, but only a primitive stage. Therefore, its primary task is to create the conditions which will make possible a more highly developed organization."
– John Foster Douglas

You can be sure that the military commanders who direct the wars of fighting nations do not operate on anarchist principles. The military as well as business organizations operate on the principle of unity of command. This means that subordinate members should all be responsible to a single commander or manager. Violation of this principle creates chaos and anarchy.

The dominant theme at the international level is that might makes right. One of the most followed theories of international policy is realism. Because there is no world authority to keep peace, it is said states should act in their self-interest, in a cool rational manner. The best way to do this is to become powerful because no other nation is going to be looking out for your interests. Realists are Machiavellian in their approach to international relations. Realism does not allow for ideals in a country's foreign policy – selfish self-interest is all that matters. Basically, at the international level, the world is a jungle where there is no law.

Close to 200 nations treat all the other nations as potential enemies that can throw them into war at any time. This fearful attitude is a normal human reaction to the existing world structure.

Municipalities usually have ordinances against carrying weapons in the city with the intent to go armed. These laws are based upon the common-sense experience that where persons are armed the chances of a person trying to settle a dispute with gun fire goes up dramatically. Practically all nations have armed themselves as a protection against the possible use of force by other nations. The governments of the nations of the world have not created a world government that would mandate national disarmament. Therefore, one would have to say that municipalities are smarter and more prudent than nations. The unregulated behavior of the world's nations is a ticking time bomb that threatens to go off at any time. Every person in the world bears partial responsibility.

Each country thinks that its arming itself is making itself safer. The reality is that all countries arming themselves makes the whole world much less safe. Each country is making decisions from its perspective and there is no government making decisions about armament from the world's perspective. If there was a judgment of the situation from the world's perspective, the present arms race would be remedied very soon. This will never be done by selfish decisions of individual nations.

This international dysfunction that is not preventing wars is the same dysfunction that exists at the world level to deal with global warming. Each country feels comfortable in polluting the air more than it should because a large part of that air pollution is blown off to other countries. When each country takes that attitude the world's air stays polluted and nothing gets done. Matters that affect the whole world should be decided by the whole world, not by selfish decisions of individual nations.

In today's anarchical international scene, nations pursue their self-interests and try to act individually to maximize their goals. Their primary motivation is survival. They build up their militaries to survive or conquer nations that are "sovereign" and are guided by their national interest through gaining power. Nations act aggressively and are preoccupied with security. The military buildup of nations leads to what is called the security dilemma.

This dilemma is created by committing to weapons and alliances to protect one's nation. Other nations are distrustful of the intentions of the nation building up their strength. This increases tensions that can cause an actual military confrontation even when neither side wants it.

The distrust of all other nations has two components to it. In an anarchy the distrust that this condition engenders is adaptive if one is destined to live in such an environment. The distrust protects us from being taken advantage of by those inclined to hurt us.

However, being trained to distrust has a number of dysfunctionalities for a healthy personality: 1) It can lead to paranoid thoughts; 2) It can make us constantly looking for danger; 3) It leads to a failure to cooperate and share information; 4) It can lead to a failure to reach an agreement with others; 5)

It can lead to depersonalization of others and 6) It can cause fear and anger. We live in a world that we cannot trust and that encourages us not to trust all throughout our lives. To be healthy we need to trust most of the persons we meet every day.

It has not been the attitude of the average individual that has thrown the human race into war. It has been largely from the attitudes and selfishness of leaders that has started wars. Enumerating the examples of this would leave no room to cover anything else in this book. The victorious nation in war generally makes the victorious war leaders the head of the conquered territory. War is often started from the top down and rarely from the bottom up. The ones on top have the most to gain and the ones on bottom do the fighting and dying. Protecting the right to make war does little for the human race.

In the anarchic international arena, it is often said that a militarily strong nation can act as a world policeman through war. In a civilized society, only the government is authorized to use force. To do otherwise is like a strong member of a nation taking it upon himself the role of policeman and kill or maiming somebody under the guise of being a policeman. In a civilized court system, no one would accept this officious violence as an excuse for killing. Because we live in an anarchy the strong nation does what it wants to do under the pretense of doing right. The weak nations just stand by and watch because they are not strong enough to stop the violence. Weak nations had no input into appointing the "policeman."

Expecting the international community to operate without rules is going against how humans are. Just as we are hard wired to depersonalize out groups, we are also hard wired to have rules within our in-group. There was no other way for small groups to function effectively through hundreds of thousands of years of human history. In small groups the rules may have been informal in nature and were generally enforced through informal means. But they had to have rules to prevent chaos and violence in the group. Humans regularly and spontaneously create rules to get along smoothly in society. We also have a need to follow and enforce rules.

Very young children can be taught to learn and follow rules. Our ability to learn, follow and enforce rules is critical to our survival as a species.

Our lack of enforceable rules at the international level is not something that is natural to us. We are not suited to anarchy. Human groups below the national level have found ways to live in harmony. Modern nations have not worked this out yet, at the international level.

Sovereignty of nations precludes enforceable rules and the world will never operate smoothly without them. Young children are more secure and happier when there are rules that are enforced. Adult humans need enforceable rules as well. Without consistently enforced rules, humans cannot focus on other important matters in life because of always having to anticipate unknown dangers.

Even arbitrary rules can put the human mind at ease because at least one knows what to expect even though it makes no sense. The worse thing that could happen is that there would be no rules. We have no rules that are enforced at the international level and disputes are not resolved through a judiciary at the international level. Is it any wonder that nations kill each other by means of war?

It is not mentally healthy to grow up in a world that makes war. The evidence is clear that growing up in a chaotic dysfunctional family creates mental problems that last a lifetime. The child becomes accustomed to defending itself against the insecurity created by chaos. They do not know how to relate to other humans unless the chaos is ever present, even throughout adult life.

In a world that allows war at any time, children and adults alike have to deal with the reality of the possibility of war at any time. This may include war with the use of weapons of mass destruction. Living through actual wars would be even worse. Anxiety disorders constitute a large part of what mental health professionals deal with. If there was a world government that prevented international murder, we have the chance of living in a world that has all of the healthy features of a stable, predictable and functional home. It might create some unemployment for psychologists and psychiatrists, but we can live with that.

Because the countries we live in are generally not anarchies, we tend to forget that internationally, the whole world lives in anarchy. In other words, our political structure is half sane and half crazy. We will all notice a big improvement in our lives when we live in a mentally healthy world. Our mistakes in the past do not need to control our future.

Ideally, political and legal agreements would be designed in a completely rational manner. However, in the real world, such agreements are the result of the circumstances and bargaining position of the parties making the agreement.

The Peace of Westphalia was also designed in an extremely unique time in history. It put an end to the 80 Years War and 30 Years War. Europe was in such a chaotic state as a result of the fighting that it appeared that there would never be any peace. The Peace of Westphalia giving all the warring parties sovereignty seemed a small concession to make considering that the parties stopped fighting. The parties went from active war and anarchy to a still anarchical state of not having a government that could prevent the nations from warring in the future. The Peace of Westphalia acknowledged the omnipotence of each country without any mechanism for resolving disputes and the United Nations perpetuated this anarchy by it calling its members sovereign. If you have sovereignty of nations with no world government, you have anarchy; and if you have anarchy, you have war. When sovereignty is done away with, a world government is possible. A world government will never allow war, just as national governments outlaw murder, and wars between groups within the nations.

The human race is in a very poor position to pass judgment on the advisability of a world government. We have a history of hundreds of thousands of years of waging war with one another, and we still do. We are used to the international world being in state of anarchy which gives indications of continuing into the future. Our adversarial relationship with neighboring countries makes us distrustful of other countries. It is difficult to be in the anarchic international environment and see clearly what is going on.

If we were a human that was from another planet who looked down on the human situation at the international level on earth, things would look radically different. Humans who are raised in a chaotic and dysfunctional environment can accept that as normal and might not feel at home in a functional and loving environment. The human race has lived with war for so long that it can feel normal. A person from another planet would look at our knowing and habitual killing of each other on a large scale as complete lunacy and lack of intelligence. We would appear to be living in an anarchical international environment that did not have a structure for resolving disputes and if disputes could not be settled agreeably, the accepted means of resolving disputes was to kill each other in war. This person from another planet would note that at the sub-national level humans had become fairly civilized, but not at the international level. This person would be perplexed at the failure to extend the rules of law to the whole world.

Generalized anxiety and paranoia are very common mental disorders for humans. When these two maladies are serious, professional help is sought. But there are many sub-clinical cases of anxiety and paranoia. Living in an anarchial world is uniquely designed to create these conditions on a wide scale. In fact, when living in an anarchy, anxiety and paranoia are adaptable psychological defense mechanisms. When we cease to live in an international anarchy, many psychologists may not have enough to do.

It is impossible to get 193 nations in the world to agree voluntarily on a disarmament or peace plan. All it takes is one nation to hold out on making such an agreement. An analogous situation from federal bankruptcy law in the United States can make the point. One alternative for a distressed debtor is to get all his or her creditors to sign a voluntary agreement about how a forbearance of creditor suits would work out and then work out a plan to implement the agreement. The problem is that every creditor has to agree to make it effective. Consequently, using the power of the Bankruptcy Court to stop the creditors is almost always required in coming up with an enforceable plan of debtor rehabilitation.

With almost 200 nations in the world, the only effective way to get real disarmament or peace is through a world government that will not allow hold out nations to mess up a good world plan. The world nations could easily agree to create a world government to stop war, but trying to get all the nations to agree every time a new issue came up will never work. The present international situation is not only anarchy but attempts at voluntary agreement on every problem is so dysfunctional intelligent people should never agree to operate like that.

The confidence of the people in the fairness of a legal system is the most important factor in obedience to the law. A sense of justice and fairness is much more important in law enforcement than force. This justice and fairness may actually exist but if it is not perceived by the people who live under a legal system it will not create compliance to the law.

Since there is no government or laws at the world level, acting according to world law is impossible. Every time a nation gets in a war with another nation, the message that is being sent is that the world is a jungle and there is no law and order. The expression of "law and order" is very important here. These two words are commonly used together because where you have effective laws you have order. Opponents of world government are quick to argue that the nations of the world will never work together because they do not now. If you believe that argument, then what is suggested is that the nations of the world should just continue to kill each other just like uncivilized barbarians. Human beings are capable of more than that. We have a proven history of learning from the past and improving our future.

Scholars agree that one of the essential requirements in defining a group of people as a civilization, is having a system of government that controls behavior. At the international level what is permissible by nations is not controlled by a government. Any nation is allowed to wage war with impunity. In other words, the world is uncivilized at the international level. Imagine that we had no police forces and people were just allowed to do anything they wanted to do, including killing other people. We would attempt to put a stop to that immediately. However, nations are allowed to do anything they want to do including waging war, and we have done nothing about it. Yet we give ourselves credit for being civilized.

A third world group of people who did not have some mechanism for curbing wholesale killing with impunity would not be considered a civilization. As the 193 plus nations of the world have no way of curbing the same thing among themselves, how are they civilized?

The following are some of those who benefit from the present international anarchy:

1. Countries who engage in cyber warfare against other countries;
2. Countries who want to expand their territory by warfare;
3. Politicians who have political appeal for persons who have a high degree of ethnocentrism and xenophobia;
4. Persons who own stock in companies which manufacture or sell war materials;
5. Corporations who manufacture or sell war materials;
6. Countries who can militarily defeat most other countries;
7. People who like war;
8. Participants in the Military Industrial Complex;
9. Military personnel;
10. Large countries;
11. Diplomats;
12. Anarchists;
13. Psychiatrists and psychologists;
14. Funeral homes;
15. Cemeteries;
16. Crematories;
17. The medical profession;
18. Rehabilitation personnel;

19. Megalomaniacs;
20. The United Nations;
21. People who are uncomfortable learning about other cultures;
22. People who hate outsiders;
23. Countries which do not want to have to follow laws;
24. Countries who want to bully other countries;
25. Murderers who use war as an example about how to behave.

The following are a few of those who are hurt by international anarchy:

1. Countries with weak militaries;
2. Pacifists;
3. Cyber warfare victims;
4. Politicians who do not appeal to persons who have a high degree of ethnocentrism and xenophobia;
5. Persons who want more of a national budget for peaceful purposes;
6. Persons who fear war;
7. Small countries;
8. Lawyers and judges who would be employed at the world level;
9. Soldiers who are wounded or die in war;
10. Families of soldiers who are wounded or die in war;
11. Legislators who would function at world level;
12. Political leaders at the world level;
13. Persons who like having laws to go by
14. Tax payers;
15. Jailers who would house murderers under a world government;
16. Persons capable of loving even strangers;
17. People comfortable learning from other cultures;

18. Persons who try to get people to settle disputes peacefully;
19. Politicians who would like to reduce taxes.

Besides war being the only means of settling disputes between nations, the threat of war is what makes small and weak nations back down against a large or strong nation. Might makes right. A good example of this is what United States President Theodore Roosevelt meant when he said, "Walk softly and carry a big stick!" It is also what is meant by gunboat diplomacy. It is also what goes on when a country has a nuclear weapon nation as an adversary.

Living in a world with war at any time is a fearful experience. War does not have to be staring us directly in the face to make us apprehensive. Humans have always made war with other outgroups. The mere fact of knowing that the world is structured that way is enough to make every person at least minimally apprehensive. Add this to the many other things in our lives that we have good reason to fear and sometimes we can be overwhelmed by fear. A few of us have generalized anxiety disorder. If there was no apprehension about war, this would have to have some beneficial effect on everyone including those with generalized anxiety disorder. It is well known that some persons have a specific fear of a nuclear holocaust. Nations with nuclear arms are not making life any easier for anyone and in particular for those who have this specific fear, simply by the possession of such weapons.

Fear is one factor that plays a part in paranoia and paranoid personality disorder. No fear of war should contribute to these disorders. Anxiety disorders also can create depression and this should be helped with world peace.

Ostensibly nations continue to try to get stronger militarily for defensive purposes and not for offensive purposes. However, there is more involved than simple defense. If a nation gets much stronger than other nations, it creates a license to militarily defeat weaker nations at will. Proactive aggressors who coolly plan and execute aggression can play the role of a bully. There has been a lot of research on bullying. Proactive aggressors in war usually do not go to war if there is a high chance of failure. They pick on the weak. Alexander "The Great" of Macedonia was raised by his father to fight wars from his infancy. His father built up his fighting machine in an unprecedented manner. When the father died, Alexander inherited his father's fighting machine with which he proceeded to conquer most of the known world. Adult bullies tend to pick on those they perceive as threats. Bullying is basically a fear reaction.

Being the strongest militarily can put a nation in the place of being the world's alpha male with all the advantages to that position. Nuclear weapon nations have a strong advantage over the rest of the world. The five victors of the Second World War (United Kingdom, United States, China, Soviet Union and France) who have vetoes in the United Nations, were the first in the world to get nuclear weapons. Having nuclear weapons against a non-nuclear enemy makes the outcome of the war a foregone conclusion. This does not mean the nuclear power will lightly use their nuclear capability, but it does mean that they will use it before being totally destroyed by the other nation. Having a strong military and nuclear weapons means you are at the top of the pecking order in the world chicken yard. Eighteenth century colonialism is a good example of military strength differences.

In our modern world many nations assert that their citizens have many rights, such as: (1) citizenship rights; (2) right to marry: (3) right to an education; (4) right to vote; (5) right to work; (6) right to free speech; (7) right to a fair trial;

(8) right to live permanently in your own country; (9) right to police protection; (10) right to fair and just conditions of work (11) right to social security; (12) right to a high standard of health. The list could go on. The right to be alive is more important than any of these rights and all of them combined. When a nation willfully lives in an anarchical world where any other nation can kill you in a war anytime it chooses, there is no way a nation can say that you will even be around to enjoy any of the rights enumerated above. Your nation is responsible for placing your life in danger by the actions of other nations. Such is the price your nation pays for insisting on national sovereignty.

Human beings are social creatures and have always been so. It is impossible to have a successfully functioning social group without some degree of discipline and respect for others. When children are two years old, they go through what is called the terrible twos. Before the child is two years old, he or she is too immature to get into any trouble and too immature to understand the meaning of punishment. So, at around two years of age the child gets into all sorts of trouble because of never having to have limits on its behavior.

The world's nations are given carte blanche authority to make war any time they do not get their way. They can act like spoiled children and not pay a price. And somehow, we are surprised when people are killed in war. The world has trained countries well to be self-indulgent and live without limits. We let nations get away with things we would never allow our children to do.

When children reach their teenage years, if they do not have a father around to set physical limits, they are very likely to be law violators. Nations in international anarchy are allowed to do anything they want and they would not be violating a law because they are not subject to laws.

Persons in the international relations field often employ the theoretical approach of realism, or political realism, in trying to come up with a strategy for dealing with the lack of a world government. Since nations exist in an anarchic environment, classical realists assert that a nation should be critical of ethical norms as primary considerations in making international decisions. Right decisions should be based on prudence considering the political consequences.

Realism has many approaches and has a long history in international affairs. Realists tend to see humans as interested in self-interest instead of morality. In an anarchy, security is of prime importance. Military enhancement is important in feeling safe. Being more powerful than adversaries is essential. Might makes right. Balancing powerful nations against each other in alliances can be effective in bringing peace.

Realists point to the failure of the League of Nations as a failure of the idealistic notion that World War Two could be prevented. The United Nations can be seen as sharing idealistic hopes for peace. Realists look at continuing wars as proof of the need for realism.

The military strength can be used in a defensive manner but it also has the consequence of powerful nations going to war against weaker ones just because it can be successful.

World government can prevent military escalation and resulting wars. Realists would then have no reason for being.

Common experience as well as modern sociological and psychological knowledge teaches us that, human beings treat persons in our in-groups vastly different from persons who are not in our in-groups. An in-group is a social group to which a person psychologically identifies as being a member. An out-group is a social group with which an individual does not identify. People prefer those who are perceived as being in their in-group as opposed to those perceived to be in their out-group. Actions of the in-group are perceived much more favorably than those of an out-group. This disparity of judgments takes place even when psychologists assign persons to different experimental groups arbitrarily in a meaningless manner.

Research has shown that in-group favoritism and out-group bias takes place at the neurological level very early in perception. Research shows that people are faster at recognizing in-group faces than in recognizing out-group faces. Persons also tend to see out-group members as more similar to each other and in-group members as more different from each other, particularly in negative characteristics.

The devaluation and dehumanizing of outgroup members are like a cocked and loaded gun ready to go off with adequate provocation.

There has been a great deal of research on human aggression. The research covers many possible causes of aggression including, but not limited to genetics, ethology, evaluation, media, neurology, hormones, social psychological causes and psychology. One thing that seems undisputed is that humans are very aggressive.

Of all other species, chimpanzees are our nearest genetic relative and just happen to be very aggressive. They use coordinated attacks just like humans do. In fact, humans and chimpanzees are the only two species in the world known to attack each other in an organized manner.

Chapter 5

"It is forbidden to kill; therefore, all murderers are punished unless they kill in large numbers and to the sound of trumpets." – Voltaire

"If the United Nations once admits that international disputes can be settled by using force, then we will have destroyed the foundation of the organization and our best hope of establishing a world order." – Dwight D. Eisenhower

The whole world tends to believe that war is inevitable. Why wouldn't it be? Humans have always been killing each other. War on a larger or smaller scale has been taking place repeatedly even before there was any history. Essentially every country spends substantial amounts of its gross domestic product supporting and arming a military for the purpose of attacking and defending itself against other countries. Historical governments and present-day governments seem helpless in doing anything about the seeming inevitability of war. The resignation to war is the main deterrent in creating a solution to war. This book hopefully will show a way out.

Humans seem to be universally susceptible to ethnocentrism, which is the applying of one's own cultural values in judging other cultures, instead of using the other culture's values as a frame of reference. This tendency establishes a disconnect between our culture and another culture. This tendency can be the first step toward the depersonalization of an enemy in war.

Humans also are commonly guilty of xenophobia, which is the hatred or fear of what is perceived as strange or foreign. The outgroups and ingroups are perceived to be in conflict. We identify with our ingroup and fail to identify with persons and cultures unfamiliar to us. Advertisers are careful to appeal to identification by trying to present their products in contexts we are familiar with. Politicians try to use identification by appearing to be like their constituents. Lawyers want jurors who can identify with their clients.

If anyone needed further proof of the human tendency to treat outsiders aggressively, just look how we have bred the dog. Just like dogs, we are generally loveable with those we are close to. When it comes to outsiders, we are just like a barking dog that instinctively barks at strangers. There are good reasons why dogs are our "best friend;" we are so much alike.

Before the invention of agriculture, about 10,000 years ago, the human species were hunter/gatherers. The human species dates back approximately 300,000 years ago. The biological antecedents to homo sapiens go back millions of years before then. During this period, hunting and gathering was the only way to feed oneself. Humans do not have and have not had the digestive tract to digest cellulose as cattle and other animals can. Consequently, there was always a shortage of food to eat. This all changed with the advent of agriculture. Although there was plenty of work in agriculture, it produced much more food for humans to eat.

Human personality was affected by hundreds of thousands of years of food shortage. It was easy to overproduce mouths to feed. Infanticide frequently became a cultural practice. Homosexuality could have been a genetic adaptation to slow down human population growth. Hunting and gathering usually necessitated moving around over great distances to obtain food. Humans became adapted to killing animals for food. Humans would come in contact with other human groups which competed for food. War was the result when food was short.

The international community has made some efforts to control "weapons of mass destruction" such as nuclear weapons and chemical warfare. However, there are plenty of other mass killing weapons such as aerial bombing and machine guns that have been with us for a long time. Those types of weapons usually do not put political leaders in danger of being killed and consequently do not generate serious attempts at eradication. As we have technologically increased our ability to kill, we have become even more immoral by killing more people in war, including noncombatants.

We do not live in the world of the past, where war has been in existence for as long as we know. We do have big brains which can adapt to new conditions and we have developed our big adaptable brain because we have successfully adapted to change in our past. No one can deny we live in a world radically different from even a few decades ago. The changes in our world necessitate that we change along with it. In preliterate human communities, we had no ability to learn from our past other than what our immediate forebearers told us. Today we have the ability to essentially comprehend all human knowledge and wisdom from a few clicks of a mouse. We are not totally dependent on current parochial customs. There is nothing in our collective knowledge and wisdom that indicates it makes any sense to continue to kill each other through wars.

The world of making wars was never planned rationally and put into practice after thought. The human race just developed that way because intergroup killing perpetuated the genes of the victors and the genes of the losers did not survive. Nobody planned it that way. It just happened that way. Communities would not allow such killing within the community and the killing essentially stopped within the group. Today we are a world community which has not learned to stop killing within our world community.

The historical and present mind set is that any nation has a right to kill persons in other countries and answer to no one for having done it. If people believe this, wars will continue because this amounts to a license to kill at will, with no punishment. When people stop thinking nations have a right to kill, the next step is agreeing to outlaw war. Only then will the killing stop.

The contradiction between the severe punishments for murder within civilized societies and the uninterrupted historical ease with which those societies go to war is no small contradiction. Is it right or is it wrong to murder your fellow human beings? The evidence seems to indicate that it just depends upon what the humans in your group think about it. Your group disapproves in the strongest of terms your killing any of them. Therefore, persons internalize the groups disapproval of killing another person in the group and along with social disapproval and legal punishment, generally refrain from killing in the group. This conclusion is consistent with many ethical philosophers who say that an expression of moral judgment is merely a statement of how that person feels about certain behavior.

Charles Darwin (1809 – 1882), Edward Westermarck (1862 – 1939) and Edward O. Wilson, would be proponents of evolutionary explanations for moral behaviors. The tendency to kill in war would appear to have a biological component.

Obviously, most all members of a country would approve of outlawing murder within that country, and each individual would be under a lot of legal and non-legal pressure not to kill within the country. However, leaders within each country could not afford to appear to stand up for foreign countries in a dispute with other countries. Even dictators need, at least to some degree, to stay on the good side of their constituents.

In the present international environment, people in out-groups cannot exert any political pressure on leaders in another country. Therefore, each country's war decisions are made without group pressure from outside of the country.

Human tendencies to depersonalize out-groups in war is likely associated with males fighting over available food with out-groups as well as killing wild animals for food for the in-group. In neither one of these situations could the in-group afford to have any empathy for what is being killed. It is not unheard of for primitive communities to eat the deceased warriors from the out-group in a war.

Nations seem instinctively to always assume their nation is right in a war, without bothering to ponder the issue to any degree. When the shooting starts on both sides of a war, it is easy to say your side is merely defending itself, because it is defending itself as well as shooting back. Who fired the first shot is long forgotten and both sides can feel it is on the moral high ground in defending itself.

When awards for valor are given out by countries, they are not prefaced by saying this particular war was justified by our side. The only issue is that we were at war and the recipient of the award killed more than his share of enemies.

Implicitly we are always right. It is not a matter of common conversation about the contradiction between awarding military honors and handing out severe punishments for murders within the in-groups. Most people never have stopped to think about such a contradiction.

Nations not only award military honors for their outstanding killers, but by not punishing its ordinary soldiers for the killing they commit, the nations are in effect rewarding their soldiers. Not punishing what would otherwise normally be punished is actually a reward. Unpunished military personnel are encouraged to continue to kill. To stop the killings, it is necessary to stop honoring killers, and stop withholding punishment for killing. This will only be done at the world level.

The only reason military persons that kill are not punished for murder is because their nation condones the killings and the international legal framework has not evolved enough to override the condonation of murder by national governments.

When a national military person works with other military personnel in their nation to kill, it amounts to a conspiracy and a conspirator is usually criminally responsible for all the conduct committed by other conspirators. Therefore, this person would be more culpable than a person acting alone.

It is no defense in criminal law that another person tells you to kill. Also, a person who plans with another person to kill is as guilty as the person who pulls the trigger.

Military personnel who have been in other wars would be considered by a limited world government to have a criminal history which would enhance their punishment and would be considered more culpable because they make their livelihood off of crime.

When two or more persons are found guilty for the same offense, a person who takes a leading role in the offense would usually be considered more culpable.

Humans became adapted to depersonalizing members of out-groups who competed with them for food for hundreds of thousands of years. All forms of life have to take in nutrients from their environment in order to live. If they cannot do this, they die. It was adaptive for small human groups to fight off competing groups.

This competition was primarily during the hunting and gathering phase of human existence which was replaced by agriculture about 10,000 years ago. Hunting and gathering supplied only enough to barely survive. Rarely would an overabundance be available. When there was the ability to store an overabundance, it was limited and the excess had to be protected from theft by other groups. During hunting and gathering, the human population was very limited in number because of the lack of food. The encounters with other groups were limited because of sparce human population.

Weapons during the hunting and gathering period were very basic and were not capable of mass destruction.

In the present-day world, humans still have the propensity to wage war but the circumstances in which they do it have rapidly changed. Humans have spread out all over the world and the world population is enormous. Agriculture has supplied humans with an overabundance of food in many areas of the world. Synthetic nitrogen fertilizer contributes to this over abundance. We have plenty of ways to store and preserve food for emergencies. Human populations expand rapidly when food is abundant. Thomas Robert Malthus made this point in his 1798 book to that effect. Hunter-gatherers constantly faced starvation, but when food became abundant, so did the population.

Agriculture has caused humans to settle down in fixed locations with strong claims on the location where they live. The population growth with agriculture has created larger groups to make for larger wars.

Today's world has weapons that can cause mass destruction. The advent of agriculture created class structures that did not exist before. Higher classes have separated themselves from lower classes and have created many modern wars to preserve class privileges. Lower classes are often the ones who fight wars.

Globalization is today a reality of life. War is still considered to be the right of each nation in the world. Fighting other groups may have started off as an adaptive response to the survival of humans. Today it is not.

Nations have a tendency to put a good face on what they do in war. They can call their military department a defense department, but will not call it an attack department. They always presume that they are on the moral high ground when they are in a war. They often attack countries half way around the world when their country's existence is not an issue. The less morally wrong country does not necessarily win the war. The country with the best killing machine wins the war; whether they are right or wrong. Stopping wars does not harm saints, but it does stop villains. Stopping wars prevents stronger nations from beating up on weaker nations. Stronger nations do not have a moral right to beat up on the weak. Let virtue reign, not military success.

People are very prone to conform to the behavior of others. An example of this was the war of the United States against Iraq in 2003. A week or two before the start of combat only about forty-percent (40%) of the persons in the United States supported attacking Iraq and sixty-percent (60%) opposed.

A week or two after the beginning of the attack by the United States sixty-percent (60%) supported the attack and only forty-percent (40%) opposed it. President George Bush alone made the decision to attack. When the attack was started, the support for it increased by the mere fact of the start of the war.

Psychologists have long known that people can be influenced by their peers to adopt certain behaviors on a largely emotional, rather than rational basis. When persons are affected by herd mentality, they tend to make different decisions than they would make individually.

Political leaders have always known how to start wars to divert the public's minds from domestic problems or help them get re-elected. Internal national disunity can almost always be solved by getting into a war with another country.

War is encouraged by the several positive psychological effects on the participants. War adds purpose to our life. It binds us together in a common enterprise to which even the non-combatants can contribute. It inspires selflessness and courage.

War also creates a dramatic shift in our thinking. We look upon the enemy as evil. Military personnel cannot think in any other way and if they did, they could not function properly in war. Wars are fought when each side has a high-minded reason for fighting, however ridiculous that reason may be.

You cannot kill someone in war at the same time you are debating in your mind who is wrong and who is right. The rightness of your cause is assumed. Added to this is the fact that if you don't kill the enemy, you will be killed by your leaders as a traitor.

In war we look upon the enemy as someone who wants to dominate us, and we are acting out of self-defense no matter who actually started the war. Purely bad motives are attributed to the enemy and good motives apply to us.

Why is it that people assume war is just normal behavior, but that murder is the most reprehensible crime there is in normal life? Before approximately 10,000 years ago, men would get together and attack people outside of their primary group of hunters and gatherers when competition for food and other resources was strong. During this period of time the hunter-gatherers were essentially egalitarian within their group. The world population was extremely small, but this war like behavior would have been in play for hundreds of thousands of years. It just seemed normal behavior. When agriculture was invented about 10,000 years ago, everything changed. People stopped roaming around hunting for food. Agriculture required that people settle down in one place to cultivate crops. Agriculture provided much more food which increased the population density. This created higher density sedentary groups of people. Communities became hierarchical with some persons having power over others who had lesser or no power. The denser the population, the more hierarchical societies became. The people in charge had strong motivations to have compliance out of the common lot of mankind, for the benefit of the leaders in charge. Ever since agriculture became widespread, the human race has become a symbiotic relationship between the aggressive-selfish and the ignorant masses. The aggressive-selfish in Egypt had the masses believing that the pharaoh was God and that he must be obeyed. War lords became kings. Wars were fought mainly for the aggrandizement of the kings and not for the benefit of the masses. William the conqueror and his warriors conquered Britain so William could inherit the kingship in England not for the benefit of the average soldier. When the Roman Empire defeated a "barbarian" territory, the ones who benefited were the aristocrats in Rome. They got the slaves and taxes that were sent back to Rome. The Roman foot soldier did not. The American Civil War was started by the slave holders in the South and was fought for their benefit, not for the benefit of the soldiers who fought and died.

Kings in Europe were successful in getting the ignorant masses to fight their many wars for the king's benefit by asserting the divine right of kings.

If wars had been fought in the last 10,000 years for the benefit of the average citizen and with the average citizen's intelligent consent, wars would have been fewer than actually happened.

In a very real sense, you could say wars have always been the product of ignorance. Ignorance of the selfish few who controlled the event because of the ignorant assumption that getting more from others than you really need makes up for what you really lack that makes you unhappy. Ignorance of the average person was responsible for buying into erroneous reasons for risking your life to benefit the powerful in their wars. War never improved anyone's life.

Within nations we have had our murderous nature largely controlled by functioning governments which have rightly discouraged killing. We cannot say that for the international world.

With democracy firmly established in the majority of the nations of the world and the data bases of knowledge at our fingertips on the internet, we cannot claim ignorance as an excuse for waging war. We need to get our heads out of the sand and stop following brainless reasons for engaging in war.

The ability of humans to make plans for the future has something to do with our propensity to plan attacks on other groups. If we did not have large brains, we would be stuck with being violent in the here and now. In other words, we are proactively aggressive because we can be. Being aggressive does not mean our aggression has to be directed to other persons. If we live through a tornado our aggression toward trying to rebuild is adaptive. If we get attacked by a wild animal, our aggression in fighting or fleeing is adaptive. Being aggressive toward the work we have to do is adaptive. Being aggressive toward the animals humans killed for food was adaptive. In many respects, the aggression we show in these areas is training for being proactively aggressive toward outgroups.

During the enlightenment the human race was quick to agree with John Locke that people should have the right to have a say so in how their governments were run. Probably the greatest reason that those ideas caught on was the increasing of fair treatment by their governments because the people were more literate. Today we have a similar situation but in a more potent form. People have so much access to learning that with a little encouragement they will demand not to be killed in wars for no reason.

We have many signs that the world looks upon itself as one community. When a ship meets a calamity on the high seas, other ships from other countries are usually quick to render aid. Responsible wealthy nations often give of their largess to render international aid for poverty relief and disaster relief. International trade is largely founded on selling what you have a differential advantage in providing and buying from other nations what they have a differential advantage in producing. Technology and learning are shared between nations with the result that the whole human race is better off. People travel the world over for leisure and peace. People immigrate freely between most nations at least on a temporary basis. The international space station is a peaceful joint effort. Many nations share a common language. There are many peaceful international nongovernmental organizations. Doctors Without Borders and the Red Cross are just two examples of this.

Nations share news coverage on a practically instant basis. Monetary and stock exchanges unite the whole world. We acknowledge a common right to travel in international waters. We extradite criminals between nations. The United Nations, despite its limitations for bringing international peace, is an honest effort to unite the world and bring world peace. The world has cooperated internationally to fight the Covid-19 pandemic and global warming. The modern Olympics is a joint effort by the whole world to live peacefully and it is not just between ancient Greek city states. The very fact we have an expression "world class athlete" shows our cooperation peacefully on an international level.

Anything that homo sapiens has been doing socially for hundreds of thousands of years is engrained in its DNA. It is not only the physical environment that molds DNA. Culture in the short run does not alter DNA. What the human race does consistently for hundreds of thousands of years is one of the environments that alter DNA.

Before the advent of agriculture, approximately 10,000 years ago, the human race rarely had an abundance of food to eat. Hunting and gathering was a meager existence. Small human groups had to wander over sometimes great distances to find enough to eat. This created conflict with other small human groups.

Human groups were already used to killing the game they found to eat. When they ran into disagreements over available food with competing groups, if starvation was the alternative, killing competing hunter gatherers was the result. Before agriculture, the human race was extremely limited in number. After the advent of agriculture, the numbers in the human race have exploded.

The present-day human personality is biologically geared to fight off human competitors for food. This basic personality is still with us even when there is enough food to go around. Aggressive competitive sports are dress rehearsals for violence against out-groups.

A high school "pep rally" is an emotionally charged affair gearing up supporters of the home team to go out and beat the other team. Support for the home team is engendered by an identification of the spectators with "our" team and disidentification with the other team. The goal is to beat the other team and make the other team lose. Winning is accomplished by outscoring the other team, by however small a margin that might be. War is conducted the same way. The two competing sides kill off each other until one side outlasts the other side by however small a margin. The objective is to kill more of them than us.

Primates, the type of mammals that include humans, apes, monkeys, and lemurs, are especially prone to kill its own kind, compared to other mammals. One of the reasons for this is that primates are territorial and social. Our closest relative, the chimpanzee, has been known to wage violent war. As the 17th century philosopher, Thomas Hobbes, asserted, in a state of nature mankind lived in a continual state of fear and in constant danger of violent death. As small bands of humans evolved into large groups, the lethal violence among humans increased. But, as social organizations and the rule of law developed, the historical rates of murder by other humans have moderated some. The innate tendency to kill our fellow humans has not, and will not go away anytime soon. But we have the ability by our political structures to control it.

Humans and chimpanzees had a common ancestor several millions of years ago. We share our violent nature with chimpanzees.

Human aggression is more proactive than reactive and this proactive trait is shared with chimpanzees. Proactive aggression is aggressive activity that occurs with no or little provocation. It can have an anger or fear reaction to an assumed threat. Reactive aggression on the other hand occurs when there is a reaction to an overt or actual threat. Proactive aggression involves a purposeful planned attack with a goal in mind. It can be done individually or in a group as in war. Proactive aggression is our most dangerous human personality trait. It is war waiting to happen.

Men are more violent than women and they have been the perpetrators of wars throughout the ages. Wars have been largely the results of patriarchal societies doing what men find comfortable in their nature to engage in. When women are aggressive, they are usually aggressive in an indirect manner which does not involve physical violence. Indirect aggression can include gossip, starting rumors, and criticism. Society rewards aggression in men more, but discourages it in women.

The tendency of men to be proactively aggressive in groups is the cause of wars. When men are predominantly in leadership positions, going to war seems a natural thing to do. Hopefully, as female leadership increases in the future, war will not seem so natural.

Chapter 6

"By the end of this decade, we will live under the first one world government that has ever existed in the society of nations ... a government with absolute authority to decide the basic issues of human survival. One world government is inevitable." – Pope John Paul, II

"We will have a world government whether you like it or not. The only question is whether it will be achieved by conquest or consent." - Paul Warburg

Ethical philosophers who assert that ethics does not have anything to do with war are just wrong. Ethical philosophy attempts to decipher what is right conduct between humans. Ethical philosophy does not have two tracts, one for us and one for them.

When small children try to settle disputes with their siblings by violence, their parents immediately put an end to it. The children are scolded and are told that violence is not allowed. When children start school, violence against other children or school personnel is not allowed. Punishment is meted out for violations. When children are older, physical violence is not allowed and violators are sent to juvenile court for appropriate punishment. Adults have been acculturated to the fact that physical violence is illegal and that violations can bring incarceration. This happens at the national and lower levels but not at the international level.

Theoretically, we have persons at the national level of government who are hopefully among our most mature and intelligent persons. Despite this fact, when it comes to committing violence between nations, mass killing of other nation's citizens is perfectly acceptable and even rewarded by the national government. Our citizens never get punished for killing the other nation's citizens. High honors are bestowed for war killings.

When fighting begins, military targets are what receive the most attention. These targets are military personnel and those activities that immediately affect the ability of the fighters to fight. Political leaders are safely hidden away somewhere else. The leaders who make the war usually do not risk their own lives. War potentially rewards those in power and punishes those who are ordered to fight. War continues to go on, and the people are acculturated to the status quo of war, and its massive killing.

People are also acculturated to the desirability of inventing more effective weapons as opposed to inventing legal measures to stop the killing, just like we do pretty effectively within countries.

Envision yourself planning a large organization that was to have bylaws to govern how the organization functioned. You had the task of drawing up the bylaws. You provided that if anyone had a disagreement with any other member, you had the right to join with people who favored your position and kill as many people who disagreed in your group. The world would think that you had lost your mind. But the world lives under the same kind of an arrangement and everybody thinks it is just normal behavior and the way the world has to work.

Which is more in the line with our sense of right or wrong: 1) the right to kill, or 2) the right not to be killed? Most people would agree the right not to be killed is more important. Unfortunately, the world internationally operates by elevating the right to kill as being more important.

It is unfair to expect our political leaders to lead the way in stopping wars. They have to spend large amounts of time in obtaining political power and running the political affairs of government. It is up to our highly educated thinkers to set a new paradigm, in the place of war as a means of settling international disputes.

During the First World War and after the First World War the expression "the war to end all wars" has been bandied about but obviously no war has ever been fought that has ended all wars. The reason there has never been a war to end all wars is the fact that people have never conceived that they have a right to not be killed in wars. When opinion leaders impress upon people their inherent right not to be killed to satisfy some nation's thirst for power, the people will demand peace and a world government to enforce that right.

The war to end wars will take place when the world's people band together to create a world government to defeat hold out nations who want to continue making wars to resolve disputes.

It is not necessary that all nations agree to end wars. When 90% to 95% of the power forces in the world band together to enforce peace, the remaining 5% to 10% will either concede defeat, or be defeated in the "war to end all wars."
Courts and government of a nation force their will on a minority all the time. It works because the courts and government of a nation have the support of the vast majority of the people. The same can and should be done at the international

level. Courts function because the almost unanimous populace realizes the government has to exist to settle disputes to prevent violence. The litigants in any one dispute would be happy to have their way but they realize the government has the overpowering ability to apply laws whether they like it or not; the government has this power because the people support it as a given and the acquiescence of the people is so basic that people don't even think about the fact they are complying. At the international level people just as automatically do not even conceive that world government is necessary or possible.

What prevents this acquiescence at the world level? It is that countries train their people to believe that law does not apply at the world level and that the only way to settle disputes at the world level is through war. Countries train their people in exactly the opposite direction from peace by honoring war heroes; thus, maintaining hate to war enemies.

When the people realize world government is not only possible but necessary, war will come to an end. People will then go to world courts with the same acquiescence that they go to existing courts to settle disputes over auto accidents.

Until people change their thinking, we will always have war. Opinion leaders have a responsibility to initiate this change and stop living in the past.

War has effects on people that are not obvious at first sight. Part of our brain acts like the brain of a reptile. War exercises the reptilian part of our brain. However, the human species has developed a large brain that has abilities and needs way beyond the reptilian part of our brain. Our complex, large brain is important in our being social animals.

It is important to our mental health that we have self-esteem. We do not improve our self-esteem by killing our fellow human beings. We improve our self-esteem by helping our fellow human beings. You can't be a healthy social animal and kill your fellow social animals.

Our brains have plasticity such that use of our brain in a certain fashion augment our brain in the direction of its repeated use. If we were not required to kill our fellow human beings, we probably would not be so predisposed to do it. Peace promotes later peace. War promotes later war.

It is a well-known fact that adverse childhood experiences create mental problems in children and in their later life. We do not like children to display bullying in school. However, internationally our countries bully other countries every time there is an international dispute. When you give children a bad example, what you expect them to do falls on deaf ears.

During the first years of life the influence of the child's mother is of utmost importance. The role of the father during those years is to allow the mother to do her important job of being a mother. When the father is under military deployment, sea duty or in actual combat, the mother has to attempt to be father and mother without doing either job well. When a father is killed in war, this situation continues and a military pension does not solve the problem.

When large numbers of soldiers or sailors are killed in modern warfare, populations become unbalanced for more than a generation. Women remain single or raise children alone.

The psychological effects of war are different from the effects of natural disasters. Since war is between human beings, there is always the feeling that the war could have been prevented. The victims of the war were the object of intervention by another human being. There is a tendency to feel that it could happen again at any time. It creates distrust of your fellow humans. It affects all families directly or indirectly.

The improved ability to kill by modern technology has increased the lives lost in modern war. There is extensive collateral damage to human life. Primitive mankind would not know what to make of all the killing. Primitive war could be only symbolic with only one skirmish with limited or no killing.

In modern warfare the deaths create labor shortage and a loss of skilled laborers. We send our best to war to die. In arms races we have always been motivated by the short-term selfish motives of the groups making the improvements in killing capacity. The long-term effect of increased killing power in the world's culture has not been a consideration. The human race would have been better off to still be fighting with sticks and stones.

Albert Einstein was disturbed by mankind's history of making and continuing to make war with highly destructive weapons. In 1932 he was appalled by the craving for power of the governing class in every nation and this class reluctance to give up its power to a world government that would stop war by legislative and judicial action. He saw as another impediment to this objective; the manufacturers of military weapons and materials. He was astounded by how these class interests could bend the masses to its will to make war. He included the intelligencia and the masses in those who could be swayed. He referred to this as a collective psychosis. He said the ruling class had the schools, press, and sometimes the church under its thumb.

Einstein corresponded with Sigmund Freud about his concerns. Sigmund Freud observed that humans are animals, just like other animals that are violent. In the early days of mankind, the strongest man was victorious. This changed when weapons came on the scene and supplanted muscular strength alone. Killing the victim was better than wounding him because future competition was eliminated and others were deterred by the example set. Freud said making the victim a slave was considered a satisfactory outcome but the master had to be careful of revenge.

To combat the strongest persons, Freud said communities must be grouped together to defeat the strong person, but it was necessary that the community be stable over time by means of emotional ties. Within the community, masters made the rules and slaves followed suit. The masters try to not hold themselves to the laws that have been made and the oppressed push for more power and the concept of equal justice for all.

Freud said besides an instinct for love, there is a counteracting instinct for hatred and destruction. He said that life arose from both love and hate. He said there is no use in trying to get rid of men's aggressive inclinations.

Freud says the proper antidote to the destructive death instinct in war is to promote emotional ties between humans. He said that whatever leads men to share important interests produces a community of feeling and identifications that discourage war. He said the world is in need of a community of men and women who have subordinated their instinctual life to the dictatorship of reason. These persons can counteract the leading of the masses toward war.

Albert Einstein in the late 1940s repeatedly came out in favor of an international governmental entity to be in charge of all national military forces. Even though this was the only path to peace, his ideas never were implemented because of opposition by the West and the Soviet Union.

Philosophical ethics has mainly concerned itself with how we treat each other within our own society and any other society we are at peace with. If we are at war with another country or think we should or could be at war with it, all our ethical considerations become irrelevant. Conventional ethics concerns itself with only part of humanity.

Aristotle was a Greek philosopher who had a lot to say about ethics. However, it was his opinion that the uncultured "barbarians" outside of Greek culture should be killed off. Aristotle tutored the son of the Macedonian king. This son was the future Alexander "the great" who conquered practically the whole known world. Aristotle was irritated that Alexander chose to work with the survivors of Alexander's killings and make them a part of his empire. For Aristotle, ethics was for "us" and not for "them."

Marcus Aurelius was a stoic philosopher who happened also to be a Roman emperor. He would be off with his Roman troops killing non-roman "barbarians" and at night would meditate on and write on stoicism.

When it comes to war, ethical philosophers seem to fall into three groups; (1) the killing in war is immoral and should not take place; (2) there are ethically defensible wars and ethically indefensible wars; or, (3) war should not be a subject that ethical philosophers deal with.

Number three (3) will be addressed here. The whole subject of ethics is all about how we as humans act in a responsible manner toward each other. If there were no humans in the world, there would not be ethics. The subject of ethics has always been of interest to humans even before the Greek philosophers. How can one say they are acting ethically when they kill the very persons they are supposed to be acting ethically towards? For ethical philosophers to say they are unconcerned with war is like a fireman remaining asleep at the fire hall while the city burns down.

There may be wars that are undertaken for a righteous cause by one of the combatants. This takes place very rarely and the righteousness of the cause is most frequently used as a rationalization for killing. Even in a "righteous war" people on both sides are slaughtered and the only ethically responsible thing is to deal with the conflict in a peaceful manner without killing.

Within countries or societies murder is considered the most immoral of acts and is punished accordingly. The populous not only realizes murder is punished severely but internalizes a moral value of the highest degree to not do it. Since when it comes to killing foreigners in war, we have no hesitation to do it, our sense of morals seems to be entirely a product of social pressures, external to an inherent sense of right or wrong. Humans seem to have manufactured moral principles that they teach their children. When we do not want you to kill us, it is wrong. When we want you to kill outsiders, it is right. The only antidote for that seems to be broadening people's identification with the whole world as a group, as well as enforcing world laws against murder anywhere in the world.

It is undeniable that murder is destructive of our society whether that is in a family or encompassing the whole world. We need to grow up and realize we owe an ethical duty to the human race as well as our next-door neighbors. If you can communicate instantly by email to someone on the other side of the world, that person is your neighbor.

The present state of the international environment concerning war is very similar to what philosophers have been saying for hundreds of years. British philosopher, Thomas Hobbes (1585-1679) was an early advocate of the social contract theory. Hobbes stated originally the human race was in a state of nature without any government. Since humans were of relatively equal physical and mental ability, they were a threat to kill or injure each other at any time. Because of scarce resources, people competed for these resources. They had to protect an image of toughness to prevent being attacked. Also, when they did acquire enough or more than enough to satisfy their desires and needs, they had to constantly defend their possession of what they had. There was no morality because everyone felt entitled to anything they could acquire, and to kill whomever they wished. Hobbes stated the life of man was solitary, poor, nasty, brutish and short.

Since there was no peace, people entered into what was essentially a social contract whereby they yielded their unlimited right to get whatever they could get and to kill whomever they wanted to kill, to a government that would settle disputes and prevent rampant violence. The government would punish those who broke the mutual agreement or social contract to forego violence.

With no present government to control war, the world finds itself in a situation very similar to the state of nature of Thomas Hobbes and subsequent social contract theorists. Present wars prove the existence of the theorized state of nature. The world is dismayed at the inability to stop war as the world is presently structured. It does not take a genius to figure out what to do. Form a limited world government! When is the world going to learn what primitive man learned thousands of years ago on a smaller scale?

Whether or not mankind explicitly formed a contract at the beginning of its history is not the important issue. The fact is that at the national and lower levels of government, the human race generally accepts governance which regulates its use of force against fellow human beings. The problem with the world at present is the fact that nations have not accepted governance to regulate their use of force.

Every human being has an ethical responsibility to some degree for every time someone is killed in war. The reason most people feel no responsibility for war is the fact people implicitly assume there is nothing anyone can do about it. If you cannot do anything about it, who, including yourself, can fault you for doing nothing?

Implicit in the world's thinking is that the world will never and can never be organized in a manner that will prevent war. Nuclear families found a way to discourage killing of other members of the family. Extended families found a way to do that. Small tribes found a way; large tribes found a way; cities found a way; countries found a way. Why is it that the world can't find a way? The way you do it is to punish warlike behavior with a government that has the support of the people for the purpose of keeping them safe and providing an enforceable adjudicatory procedure for settling disputes between nations. Police will always be necessary in society and they need to be at an international level as well as the national and lower levels of government. National military forces will not be necessary or required when the world government enforces an outlawing of violence just like each country already does at home in their own country.

Ethical philosophers have considered the issue of whether there is a moral difference between doing harm and merely allowing harm. Even those who find a moral difference do not seem to be saying that allowing harm has no moral implications. Consequentialists say that the moral quality of an act depends only on consequences. These philosophers believe that doing harm is no worse than merely allowing harm. An example of allowing harm would be letting scores of children in impoverished countries die of malnutrition when it was possible to save them. Another example of allowing harm would be allowing future wars when a limited world government could prevent this. There is absolutely no reason a world government could not essentially eradicate war in the same way national governments have essentially eradicated war within their own territories. A person who does not push for a world government to eradicate wars is committing an immoral act of non-feasance. Opposing such a limited world government is essentially saying "let my country continue to kill people in war."

The status quo is clear. There has been rarely interrupted war all over the world throughout human history and before recorded history. There is no indication that this will stop and the League of Nations and United Nations have only trimmed around the edges of homo sapiens' biggest problem. Humans have used their big brains not to solve the real problem but to make weapons even more powerful and dangerous. We have been focusing on trying to win wars instead of stopping them. In retrospect, the human race looks like fools that cannot solve the big problem.

When the public around the world realizes that war is not inevitable and there is a solution, the world will change for the better. Posterity will look back on the 21st century and say we finally came to our senses.

The human race has been struggling with what is the right ethical behavior for thousands of years. Humans are social animals and right conduct first and foremost affects other human beings. It is impossible to effectively argue that killing the object of your morality is not a moral issue. Ethical conduct involves doing right by your fellow human beings. Destroying your fellow human being is not ethical or moral conduct. Structuring your world such that your fellow human beings are destroyed by war is not ethical conduct.

Humans have always had disagreements that could lead to violence. Small groups found ways to resolve these disagreements in manners that preserved the group. As groups increased in size, various methods were used to adjudicate conflicts, such as councils of elders, assembly of the people, etc. If there were not successful developments of conflict resolution, the group would no longer exist as a unit; with every increase in the size of the social unit, the adjudication of disputes continued. Each nation has its own method of resolving disputes within its borders. When one goes beyond the borders of each nation, the world has no binding mechanism for dealing with international disputes.

It is commonly accepted that the primary means of prevention of war are diplomacy and arms control. As important as these are, it is clear that they have been inadequate to bring peace to the world. They both suffer from the same problem. Diplomacy depends totally upon trying to cajole another country into not going to war. There is no world government to prevent the parties from going to war. Arms control is also completely dependent upon agreement on each country's part to limit their armament. As each country is afraid other nations will be militarily stronger than them, disarmament is hard to sell.

The world's political experience in both, the 20th and 21st centuries shows clearly that narcissism, untempered by a world government, can cause major world problems.

Two other personality disorders can create real problems when the world depends wholly on voluntary resolution of disputes over war issues. They are paranoid personality disorder (about 4% of persons) and anti-social personality disorder (about 2 to 4 % of persons).

Another personality trait of political leaders could present problems for consensual resolution of disputes at the world level. Political leaders have to have a high degree of assertiveness. Unless they happen to have inherited a royal throne, they got to where they are by pushing themselves forward and in the case of revolutions, likely to have been a victorious warrior. This personality trait is likely not the best for making cool, rational judgments in resolving disputes.

The world needs an adjudicative process for nations to resolve disputes no matter what the personalities of the parties' representatives and no matter whether the representatives make adequate rational assessments of their respective rights under world law.

Having a world government that would prevent war is not a new idea. A few others have envisioned such a government for hundreds of years. Obviously, their vision has never come to pass. However, the world has never before evolved closer than it has now to needing or having such a government.

If a nation objects to moving in the direction of having a world government that would outlaw war, it would be in effect saying it should continue to have the sovereign right to wage war for whatever reason it should want to do it. Once it concluded the war, it would not have any punishment for premeditatedly killing thousands of persons. It would be placing itself in the position of being a hypocrite. On the one hand it considers it wrong to kill another person in its own country and being punished severely for doing that, and on the other hand a country can kill with impunity anytime it wants.

Persons who object to a world government would use the argument that the world's nations would never be able to be friendly enough to work together in a world government. Social psychological research and experience tells us otherwise.

In 1954 social psychologist, Muzafer Sherif, published a study that involved two groups of boy scout campers who did not know each other. Over time, the two groups developed hostilities to each other. When it happened that they had to work together on a common project, they became more co-operative and their conflict resolved. This study led to further research into conflict resolutions through shared goals and identity.

During the second world war there was extreme hostility on the part of Germany, Italy and Japan, and the countries that were allied against them. This hostility does not exist today. In fact, France and Germany are members of the European Economic Union. France and England fought each other for 100 years in the Hundred Years War. Today they have an underground tunnel under the English Channel connecting their two countries for peaceful purposes. Europe was literally torn apart by the Thirty Years War, and Eighty Years War until these were resolved in 1648 by the Peace of Westphalia. Today Europe is joined together in the European Economic Union.

Humans have the ability to get along together when they cease killing or threatening each other. Just as different political subdivisions within nations almost always get along and work together, the world can likewise.

Human psychological health is largely based upon harmony within families. Our psychological health is further improved when we have good relations with our extended families and the people we interact with regularly. It is impossible to have too many persons treat us well. If we join with our whole human family and take pride in our human family, all humans will benefit. If we can create harmony within our nation, we can do it in our world. If we can identify with our nation, we also have the ability to identify with the human race. After all, we appear to be on a planet that alone has human life. We have come a long way in getting where we are and can be proud of that. If young children are taught to love all humans, when they are grown, they might do just that. Children have a remarkable ability to act like they are taught by their parents and cultures.

If we do it right, we can create empathy for the whole human race and not just our own group. If we instill this kind of empathy, we can avoid what psychologists call moral exclusion, which means we withdraw human and moral rights from other groups and refuse them justice and respect. If ethical standards are applied only to our group, homicide, exploitation and oppression are not far behind.

Persons who are hesitant to support a world government are really saying that law enforcement officers are unnecessary. At the international level we do not have law enforcement officers to enforce world law, and nations can kill at will. If law enforcement officers are unnecessary, why is it that practically all nations have such officers? Without such law enforcement officers, there would be everybody trying to kill and rob everybody else.

These same persons who object to world government, would say that they do not want to sit on world juries to decide world cases. How could anyone object to that?

The whole human species has become acculturated to war because it has been so common, and we do not think of the possibility that it does not have to happen. We take the air we breathe for granted and we don't even think about it. We are like fish who take water for granted. We have been so acculturated to war that we don't even see the contradiction between making it a moral issue for a person killing his neighbor and not making it a moral issue about killing someone in war. When we humans become acculturated strongly about something, we just flip off the switch in our brains. Flipping the switch about war has all the indications of being a world-wide handicap that prevents us, under the conditions we live in today, of solving the problem of war.

Unless the world blows itself up with nuclear weapons, it is certain that the world is moving in the direction of a world government over time. The world is just like it was when hunter-gatherers settled down in one place and took up agriculture. When that happened, it was necessary to have a government to deal with the close interaction between persons. It was impossible to function without government. Our present technological advances and globalization makes it mandatory we have a government to sort out problems at a world level. It is not a matter of whether we will have a world government, but when. Let's hope it is before we completely kill each other.

What is proposed in this book is a federal world government that will at least keep us from killing each other. There are plenty of other reasons to have a world government at this very moment. Those other reasons are important but not near as urgent or important as stopping war.

The almost 200 nations in the world today are analogous to a large tribe or agricultural community that created a government to manage the interactions between persons so that the government had a monopoly on the use of violence to prevent violence between members or groups within the community. If we have not learned the wisdom of that, we have not progressed in the last few thousands of years; we have regressed.

A federal world government could easily be limited in its powers to preventing war and not be granted the power to do much else.

National space agencies are seriously planning for permanent colonization of the moon and mars. If and when these settlements become a reality in a significant way, what nations from earth are going to "own" the moon and mars? Are we going to have another world war to decide who gets possession of what? Are we going to recognize national sovereignty in the settlement on the moon and mars? Is it going to be the earth versus mars or the moon? There are many other issues related to the moon and mars. Are we going to fight over these issues like the barbarians that we act like now, or are we going to decide these issues peacefully with a government?

At the present time we have only a handful of nations who put satellites into orbits around the earth. They are USA, France, Japan, China, UK, India, Russia, Ukraine, Israel, Iran and North Korea.

There certainly are going to be many more as technology improves and becomes more available. Loading a large satellite with a nuclear or other bomb and coasting it into a nation of choice would be easy to do. There are almost 200 nations in the world and if these nations are considered sovereign, they would have the right to attack any nation they chose from space. Only fools would acknowledge national sovereignty and live under anarchy under these circumstances. But that is what we do.

Since private corporations are getting geared up to do space travel, the danger of violence is not limited to the nations of the world, but private parties all over the world going forward will also present a threat.

Chapter 7

"Our modern states are preparing for war without even knowing the future enemy." – Alfred Adler

"The tragedy of war is that it uses man's best to do man's worst." – Harry Emerson Fosdick

People can only think of one thing at a time. Every moment you are thinking about war; about planning and preparing for war; and, actually fighting a war; the less time you have for creating the right conditions where war is prevented. Persons who oppose world government want to continue thinking about war and not thinking about preventing war. They want to continue to ignore the problem and save themselves the mental energy required to find a real solution.

The anachronistic nature of the United Nations with its guarantee of sovereignty to its members and its veto power to permanent members of the Security Council, is a prime example of the sociological concept of cultural lag. If national sovereignty and the veto power of the permanent members of the Security Council ever made any sense when created, they surely do not make sense now. Cultural lag is where material culture changes but the non-material culture, which is slow to change, lags behind. Non-material culture refers to the belief system of people such as ideas, religions, rules and tendencies to act in certain ways. There are many material culture changes which make having a world government feasible and advisable, but people have a hard time adjusting to these changes. For instance, the internet has been around for a very few years, but this invention has revolutionized the world and makes world government highly feasible. Another example is nuclear weapons which cause international danger. Intercontinental ballistic weapons are another example. The world is radically different than it was in 1648 when national sovereignty was essentially created. The rate of change in the world is expanding and not stagnant or decreasing. The human species, being psychologically resistant to change, is clinging to its outdated political institutions which create the continued unnecessary killing of fellow human beings.

For about two-hundred years (27 BC to 180 AD), the Roman Empire was known for maintaining peace in its large sphere of influence. It governed its provinces but allowed each to make their own laws. Its maintenance of military control prevented most all wars in the empire. This phenomenon was called Roman Peace. There have been a few other periods in history that have been similar to this peace within an empire. These periods of peace demonstrate what can be done for peace when an entity is in control that prevents wars.

One of the best arguments for a world government is based upon the fact that well over half of the national governments of the world are democratic. Democratic nations can make mistakes, but they have the ability to correct those mistakes. The long-term trend is toward more democracies and less autocracies. When national sovereignty came about at the peace of Westphalia in 1648, there were essentially no democracies in the world. There was not even the philosophical rationale for democracy until the Enlightenment which postdated 1648. Democracy has proven itself in the recent centuries to be workable and desired by people.

Providing for adjudication of disputes is a relatively inexpensive endeavor. For example, the Defense Department of the United States takes up approximately 16.6% of the annual budget expenditures. The Federal Judiciary takes up 0.2% of the budget expenditures. Imagine what would happen if the courts, lawyers and police were eliminated. The country would self-destruct. That is what the judicial systems do: they prevent violence over disagreements. We can send rockets to deep outer space and enjoy the advantages of the internet but we haven't been smart enough to provide a judicial system for the world and thereby prevent war.

Well, this is what the reality is at the international level. Countries have no peaceful way to settle their disputes so war is the only option.

A more is an unenforceable custom that is generally agreed upon. It does not have the force of law even though a violation of the more may put the violator in a position of public or private disapproval. A law, on the other hand, always has a sanction by the government for violations. If there is no sanction, there is no law.

Because countries of the world have not seen fit to prohibit wars and back up that prohibition with sanctions, they are saying that they think your parking ticket is more important than outlawing the mass murders in war.

The printing press with movable type was invented in 1440, but it took almost 400 years before this invention reached the whole planet. Before the printing press, the average human was unbelievably ignorant by today's standards.

The countries involved in the Peace of Westphalia were mostly kingdoms. Kings got their positions by being successful warlords who defeated all their rivals. They certainly were not on any moral high ground which justified their being granted sovereign powers. Recorded history is dominated by ingroup/outgroup violence and ignorance. Human groups were a symbiotic relationship between the aggressive, selfish leaders and the ignorant masses of people who did what was best for the dominant leaders.

For example, pre-Columbian indigenous Americans believed their rulers were divinely ordained to lead them. Ancient Egypt was also structured on a similar basis. At the time of the Peace of Westphalia, the divine right of kings was also widely believed in, which kept the masses cooperating with those who directed them. The divine right of kings worked great for the kings and this idea was only possible with a grossly ignorant populace.

Every nation in the world that exists today is a product of historical wars that shape its present territorial limits. Borders are nothing but dividing lines where one group's influence stopped and another's began. There is nothing set in nature about national territories. Nations exist only as the result of violent historical events.

Nation-states never really existed before the Peace of Westphalia in 1648. Before then, human groups existed in the forms of families, tribes, empires, villages, city states, etc.

To give sovereign status to the 193 nations of the United Nations is pretending that a concept that was invented in 1648 should control the world forever in the future. The human race did not become all knowing in 1648 when it had somehow missed this wisdom in the hundreds of thousands of years before then. Sovereignty was maybe a useful concept when it was invented, but it has little usefulness today. The world cannot go on allowing 193 political units to do whatever they want to do without the rest of the world having a say so in what they do. The world has an interest in suppressing pre-meditated murder on a grand scale by any of the 193 countries in the world that is inclined to do it. A country that does that is more morally wrong than your neighbor who lies in wait and kills you when you come out your front door.

The world needs to decide whether murder is wrong or right. As the world stands now it cannot give you an answer. Within a nation, it is considered wrong in a serious sort of way. Between nations, murder is applauded and the more you do of it, the higher you are honored.

The world has already been evolving in the direction of ignoring national sovereignty in some respects. Globalization has moved in the direction of making nations more interconnected and national boundaries more transparent. The most rapidly growing parts of industry and business are international. National internal affairs are shrinking and voluntary relinquishment of national sovereignty is growing.

Economically and technologically, the world is becoming more interconnected and people are growing accustomed to this natural evolution. Doing away with national sovereignty is less and less a strange concept every day. Regional voluntary associations are growing all the time. National sovereignty does not have to be an all or none matter. The European Union is a good example of giving up partial sovereignty. EU members give up national sovereignty on certain economic and social issues but not on most all military matters. In general, this has seemed to work well. The ideas in this book contemplate a relinquishment of part of sovereignty by the nations of the world but not all sovereignty. However, this book contemplates basically the opposite of what happened in the EU. What is urgently needed in the world is a relinquishment of sovereignty in military matters but not necessarily in other matters of national interest.

In 1648 nations did not have nuclear weapons. They did not have intercontinental ballistic missiles. There were no self-propelled submarines or torpedoes. Shrapnel had not been invented. Rifling on guns was not practical until the 19th century. In 1648 there were no repeating firearms. Firearms had to be loaded by the muzzle of the guns. There were no machine guns. Chemical weapons had not been invented in 1648. There were no airplanes in wars. There were no tanks used in wars. There were no electronically guided weapons. There were no rockets into outer space or anti-satellite missiles. There were no drones. No laser weapons technology was available in 1648. The internal combustion engine and steam engine had not been invented.

At the present time, nations in the world have nuclear weapons, intercontinental ballistic missiles, chemical weapons, and all sorts of other high technology weapons. In the 16-hundreds, when the concept of national sovereignty was originated, the world was making the transition from fighting wars with swords and arrows to muskets and cannons. War was mostly fought with hand-to-hand combat, and the few firearms that were used were not very accurate.

The prevailing paradigm of national sovereignty is an anachronism in the 21st century. Its origination in 1648 through the Peace of Westphalia was made under completely different circumstances than exist in the 21st century. The countries involved in the Peace of Westphalia, which settled the 80-Years War and 30-Years War, were monarchies. The wars that were settled were basically religious wars between Catholics and Protestants. After practically destroying Europe, it was decided that each monarch could determine the religion of the people within his kingdom.

Later in the 17th century and into the 18th century, the world experienced what was called the age of Enlightenment. Philosophers led the way with progressive ideas that were based on reason and not on dogma and authority. These ideas have profoundly influenced the world to the present day. Included were ideals such as progress, fraternity, constitutional government, separation of church and state, and human freedom. Prior to 1648 the world, suffering from massive illiteracy, was sold on the idea of the divine right of kings. Consequentially, selfish kings ran their areas of influence for their own selfish interests and drug the average persons along with them to fight their wars, in power struggles with other monarchs.

Today, few governments are monarchies. Few heads of government are now considered sovereign by the people. Most of the world's nations are democracies. Literacy is widespread around the world. Knowledge on practically everything important is just a few clicks of a mouse for anyone with a personal computer. Humanity, not kings, are in control of the world. The world, including the United Nations, need to stop ceding sovereign authority to nations to make war, at will, and with impunity.

Imagine what would happen if parents decided that they were going to raise their children with the assumption that the children have supreme authority over themselves. The children would never make it to adulthood and if by chance they did, they would be criminals who were not fit to live in a social species' culture.

Giving sovereignty to 193 nations has the same effect on the nations as on children. There is not one person alive who was alive when the idea of sovereignty was originated. The whole world has grown up with the idea that every nation was all powerful, and the only way to resolve differences between these omnipotent countries was to kill off the country your country had a disagreement with.

Imagine what would happen if people in tribes had asserted supreme authority over themselves. The tribes would have disowned any people that did this, because it would have made it impossible to live in a social culture as humans must. Of course, the obvious thing happened and that is that the tribe members consented to decision making authority by a member or members in the tribe.

When cities were formed after humans took up agriculture, the decision-making process became more complex and disputes were resolved without individuals or groups being allowed to claim supreme authority over themselves like "sovereign" nations claim.

When nations were formed almost four-hundred years ago, cities were not allowed to claim supreme authority over the city.

Sovereignty is generally defined as supreme authority within a territory. When the United Nations recognizes sovereignty of nations it is in effect giving a nation the right to possess the characteristics of a person that has a narcissistic personality disorder. Someone who has this disorder has at least five of the following characteristics:

- overinflated sense of self-importance;
- constant thoughts about being more successful, powerful, smart, loved or attractive than others;
- feelings of superiority and desire to only associate with high-status people;
- need for excessive admiration;
- sense of entitlement;
- willingness to take advantage of others to achieve a goal;

- lack of understanding and consideration for other people's feelings and needs;
- arrogant or snobby behavior and attitudes

This is not to say that a country will display all of these characteristics, but that being considered a sovereign gives a license to a nation to act like a narcissist if it chooses.

Narcissism is a disorder because it does not allow the individual to perform adequately in a social human environment. If a nation acts like a narcissist, trying to get the nation to act reasonably in negotiations about preventing a war is a waste of time.

Personality disorders are almost impossible to treat successfully. Since up to five percent (5%) of persons have a narcissistic personality disorder, it is reasonable to assume that out of 193 nations in the United Nations, some persons will be negotiating over possible war with no chance of a successful outcome.

In 1648 none of the nations that resulted from the Peace of Westphalia where the concept of sovereignty was basically originated, were democracies. Modern democratic nations got their start after the mid-17th century. In 1648 the world's nations were largely monarchies. In 1900 there were no nations in the world with universal suffrage. In 2000 62% of the world's nations were liberal democracies with universal suffrage. The long-term trend is people of the world taking control of their political destiny. Throughout history, wars have mostly been caused by the decisions of selfish leaders and not so much by the people themselves. A democratic world generally sees little reason for nations to kill each other. The people can effectuate this reality by a limited world government that does not allow war.

In every war between sovereign nations, each nation is both right and wrong in resorting to war. If you ask nation A it will tell you it is right and nation B is wrong. If you ask nation B it will tell you it is right and nation A is wrong.

Sovereignty is not a useless concept. The world government should be considered sovereign. It would have none of the downsides to treating almost 200 nations as if they were sovereign. The sovereign world would not bump heads with other sovereign worlds that we have no evidence exist. The sovereign world would have no desire to attack other worlds. It could demand that the world live in peace and it would live in peace or nations would be subject to world-imposed sanctions. Expecting almost 200 sovereign nations to live in peace has never happened and will never happen.

In 1648 science as we know it did not exist. It was mainly after that date that science really got started. Today science has hundreds of disciplines and sub-disciplines in natural science which can be broken down into physical science and life science. These sciences got their start mainly after 1648 and before social science got its start. Today social science has over 250 disciplines and sub-disciplines.

Our knowledge of the world and the human race is so much greater than was ever imagined in 1648 that it is hard to take seriously a concept that was invented around 1648 to stop decades of destruction by war in Europe. When the concept of national sovereignty originated in 1648 at the Peace of Westphalia, the idea of nations was a work in progress. Earlier in history there was not necessarily what we think of as nations. For example, what we think of as the nation of Germany did not even exist. What existed instead was a large number of warring groups that had not melded yet into the nation of Germany. The parties that settled their differences at the Peace of Westphalia were mainly monarchies which usually had the misguided presumption of the divine right of kings with absolute power. In fact, the word sovereign means the chief of state in a monarchy and a monarch is the absolute and single ruler of a state. So, in 1648 sovereign did not even mean what we have existing in the world today. Today we have 44 monarchies in the world out of approximately 200 nations. Out of these 44 monarchies, only 6 monarchs have absolute power. Thirty-one have monarchies that are limited by constitutions.

Somehow the international diplomatic community has transferred the concept of sovereignty over to the approximately 200 nations in the world today despite the fact that 167 of these nations are democracies instead of monarchies. Treating the approximate 200 nations in the world as if they have absolute powers is what keeps war in the world. The average person no longer thinks national government officials are destined by God to have absolute power, but somehow those officials have not gotten the message. How can we treat national leaders as ordained by God when we can throw them out of office at the next election?

One year after the Peace of Westphalia, King Charles the First of England, Scotland and Ireland from 1625 was executed in 1649 after fighting with parliamentary forces. He was tried for treason and convicted. Charles I was a staunch believer in the divine right of kings and would not back down from this viewpoint and as a result the parliament executed him. Before Charles I, his father, James I was a strong believer in the divine right of kings when he reigned from 1603-1625. The idea of the divine right of kings was pretty much history after the Glorious Revolution in Britain (1688-1689). After the Glorious Revolution, English philosopher, John Locke, published in 1689 Two Treatises of Government which argued against the divine right of kings and for the social contract theory of government. He stated everyone had equal and natural rights to freedom from domination by others.

Historical periods are generally not very specific in their beginning and ending dates. However, the seventeenth century was a real turning point in history. In prior centuries, Europe was in the Middle Ages that was dominated by the catholic church and feudalism after the fall of Rome. The Middle Ages went from the fall of the Western Roman Empire in the 5th century to the late 15th century. Philosophy during this period dealt primarily with Christian doctrine.

As part of the Renaissance, the world went through the scientific revolution in which from around 1543 to 1687 various scientists transformed the world. Francis Bacon (1561-1626) is credited with first defining the scientific method. Instrumental persons were, René Descartes, Nicolaus Copernicus, Isaac Newton, Galileo Galilei, and Johannes Kepler. When the Peace of Westphalia established the precedent for national sovereignty in 1648, Isaac Newton, the chief refiner of the modern scientific method, was only 5-years old.

When the Peace of Westphalia took place, kings and emperors ran countries. People were largely illiterate. That is not the case today. Today educated people generally rely on the scientific method. Humanity is generally literate. Sovereignty was a concept that was dysfunctional. It was dysfunctional in the 17th century for the following reasons:

1. The violent history of monarchs was well known and the violent history of the human species throughout the history of the world was well known. Wars were bound to happen on a regular basis. That is what has happened.

2. The divine right of kings was a well-entrenched rationalization for getting the population to be compliant to all the

selfish wishes of monarchs. The only way this doctrine was put forth was because of the symbiotic relationship between selfishness and ignorance.

3. Sovereignty of nations in 1648 was a political compromise to get warring monarchs to put their weapons down and stop the killing in the 30-years war and the 80-years war. It was not a wise decision in the long run because it created an international anarchy that exists to this very day.

4. No dispute resolution procedures were put in place to resolve disputes between nations.

5. The people had no voice in the peace treaty. Only the monarchs made the decisions which suited themselves. The decision for sovereignty was not legitimate according to democratic standards.

6. The decision for sovereignty authorized killing of humans on the whim of a nation without any punishment for doing so.

7. Sovereignty of nations was decided upon without any scientific knowledge of human behavior.

8. Sovereignty between the parties to the Westphalian Peace was only a private agreement that had no relevance to the rest of the world.

There are a number of reasons why national sovereignty is unwise today:

1. Globalization has created a situation where there is more interaction between nations that demands international regulation.

2. Global warming is something that cannot be dealt with successfully by approximately 200 different independent nations.

3. Weapons of mass destruction threaten all nations.

4. The United Nations is firmly entrenched in the paradigm of international anarchy.

5. Pandemics cannot be dealt with successfully by individual nations.

6. The United Nations and voluntary regional associations of nations have proven that nations can sit down and talk rationally and solve some problems.

7. There has never been in the existence of the human species a time when humans did not kill each other.

8. Modern humans are largely literate and have at their disposal unbelievable amounts of accumulated learning readily at hand.

The failure of the world's nations to form a world government to outlaw war has created an international anarchy. Anarchism comes in several forms but basically this political theory is distrustful of authority and power. Anarchists do not believe in state power and believe each person should be free to relate to others by non-coercive consensus building.

The 193 nations which make up the United Nations obviously do not operate internally on anarchist principles. To say that an organized nation that is a member of the United Nations is anarchist is a contradiction in terms. A sovereign nation is highly organized and has theoretically ultimate power over its citizens.

However, these same nations that do not exist in an anarchist world are very comfortable with anarchy at the world level. They pride themselves in their sovereign right to go to war with whomever they please. This asserted right creates anarchy in international relations. These nations want the best of all possible worlds. They want to coerce their citizens but do not want anything or anybody to coerce them. The international anarchy they create is not because they believe it is philosophically or morally correct. They create this anarchy because it makes them all powerful. The downside is the lives lost in war. But it is not the powerful who are sent to die in war, so anarchy continues.

The subject of ethics has to do with our proper relations toward our fellow humans. If there are approximately 18 humans alive for every one alive when the concept of national sovereignty was accepted as the paradigm for the world, the subject of ethics is approximately 18 times as important as before. We need to be 18 times more careful with our prescriptions for working together. National sovereignty does not make the grade.

Chapter 8

"Nationalism is an infantile disease. It is the measles of mankind." - Albert Einstein

"War will exist until that distant day when the conscientious objector enjoys the same reputation and prestige that the warrior does today." - John F. Kennedy

"Politics is war without blood, while war is politics with blood." - Mao Tse-Tung

If one accepts this conclusion of Mao Tse-Tung, then war has the same purpose as politics and politics has the same purpose as war. What people need to decide is what is the more moral of the two forms of politics. Acquiescence in a system of warfare constitutes a person's answer to this question. Every human life carries with it a recommendation of how to live to the next generation. Every person shares responsibility for how the future generations turn out.

Humans can consciously and/or unconsciously compensate for perceived personal deficiencies. Many times, this turns into overcompensation. Leaders of a nation can engage a nation in national overcompensation. Both, Alexander "the great" and Napoleon were of short stature and are considered to engage in power compensation because of this fact. Over compensation can drag a nation into behavior that has devastating consequences in the world and that have no rational reason for taking place.

National idealization can turn members of a nation who are otherwise rational individuals into fanatics who oppress adversaries and non-believers.

The human species historically had been unaware of the existence of our unconscious mind. This changed around the start of the 20th century with the work of Sigmund Freud. Hypnosis had its beginning around that time and slightly before that time. The development of the knowledge of the unconscious mind and hypnosis coincidentally came along when powerful deadly weapons were changing the nature of warfare. It has been learned how to manipulate and program the unconscious mind of masses of people for the benefit of those doing the manipulation. Subliminal messaging is just the most obvious of these methods. This makes the possession of the highly destructive modern weapons an increased danger to the world because minds can be controlled both within and outside of nations, who in essence have a license to kill at will.

If one wants to drive a car, a license is required because cars can be dangerous. However, war is many times more dangerous than cars and no license is required or standard set to prevent war. To have a license to kill in war all that is required is that you exist as a nation.

It is nothing short of immoral what intelligent, educated adults all around the world allow to happen to children in war. No one has ever merited a high military honor from defending against an army of children. Unless children are forced into a combat situation where they are made to fight, they are always defenseless victims of war. Children affected by war are not allowed to grow up in a loving stable environment which is necessary for their emotional and psychological development.

History is going to judge mildly our early human and prehuman ancestors for violence and killings that took place prior to the invention of agriculture because of the scarcity of food in hunting and gathering communities. The alternative would have been death from starvation. Agricultural groups had generally more food and they started our accumulating wisdom through generations by a means other than of word of mouth. Hunter and gatherer's ignorance could easily be forgiven. Even after writing was developed, accumulating wisdom through the generations was not available to the common man before the invention of the printing press in 1440. Violence in war toward outgroups could easily be forgiven because of this ignorance. History is not going to be very forgiving of the 21st century for fighting to kill each other in war when knowledge and wisdom are readily available. Persons in the 21st century have no excuse for fighting to kill each other. Failing to use our large brains is no excuse.

The people of the world need to get away from the idea that they are not responsible for the killing around the world. Europeans were clearly not responsible for the military killings in the formation of the Inca empire in South America because they did not even know that America existed. The Chinese were not responsible for Viking invasions in Europe between 800 – 1000 because if they knew of it at all, it was by long distance, by slow word of mouth. Before the invention of the steam engine, learning of information from wars in other parts of the world was only transmitted by ships sailing over the oceans very slowly. Very little was learned and there was little ability to do anything about it. Today we live in a vastly different world which creates more responsibility for what happens in the world. Land line and cell telephone services exist. The internet exists. Intercontinental passenger air flights exist throughout each day. Satellites beam electronic information to us all day and night. With increased information and increased ability to positively affect our social and natural environment, we have a greater moral responsibility to correct injustices. If that means altering the concept of national sovereignty, so be it. We are quite willing to reap the benefits of technological advances but are hesitant to become morally responsible for more. You can't have one without the other. We interact with others all over the world like one human family. We need to recognize the fact that we should treat others as extended family members. One would be really challenged to find any philosopher, psychologist or psychiatrist who has ever recommended war or murder as an effective means of achieving human happiness. These are persons who have considered human well-being in a thoughtful manner. Despite the fact that none of these persons have ever even considered that war or murder ever came close to being worthy of consideration as a candidate for achieving happiness, the human race has continued through its history to go to war and murder each other. Socrates is quoted as saying "the unexamined life is not worth living." Humans have a need to find an internal state of personal well-being. In their failure to achieve that state they repeatedly make the ignorant assumption that if they just lash out and control things and persons outside themselves, the internal disfunction (unhappiness) will just magically go away.

At the national and sub-national level, the world has done a decent job of mandating that humans curb their most dysfunctional behavior such as murder and other crimes. The problem with the world in the 21st century is they have not seen fit to do this at the international level.

The educated person in the 21st century is doing no favor to the ignorant persons who still believe in war as a solution to their problems, by failing to have a world government. Having a world government to stop war is the first step toward moving the world in the direction of achieving happiness through the only means it will ever be achieved: nonviolence.

Humans have been considering the concept of justice for at least two and one half thousand years. Justice hopefully is the end product of a thoughtful analysis of what is lawful and equitable treatment between human beings. Philosophers who have contributed to this concept have included Plato, Aristotle, Augustine, Aquinas, Hobbes, Kant, Mill and Rawls, among others. When a legal system approaches an approximation of a good faith effort to achieve justice, it has the respect of the governed. The governed are then more inclined to follow the law. The perception of legitimacy is more important in following the law than actual enforcement of the law through force.

Every time a war takes place, throughout history and in the present world, there is an outcome that has nothing to do with justice. The outcome is determined by which country was the most successful in killing the other country. The winner has no real legitimacy, only power. The winners of the second world war are in firm control of the United Nations and this has existed since 1945. The United Nations continues to allow nations to kill each other and every time this happens, the status quo changes, not based upon an attempt to reach a just result, but upon the results of a war.

"Successful crime is dignified with the name of virtue; the good become the slaves of the impious; might makes right; fear silences the power of the law." Lucius Anneals Seneca

Our schools do their best to stop bullying in schools, but their efforts are teaching a different lesson than national governments. How do you get school children to stop bullying when bullying is taken for granted at the international level? This is just another example that the government is allowed to do things that people cannot do. Is bullying right or wrong?

National governments who are reluctant to give up part of their sovereignty to cede power to a world government should model the behavior which they impose on the world, in their own nation. They should say to all of their subordinate states and provinces as well as all their cities, that they are sovereign and that the national government cannot do anything to affect their respective territories. War between these parts of the nation would be legal and no one would be guilty of murder in any of the wars. No binding adjudicative process would be set up to resolve any disputes. Of course, these things would never be done because it would destroy the nation.

The human race flatters itself by thinking it rises above killing. We use the word "humane" to express the quality of mercy, compassion or kindness, despite having wholesale slaughtered our fellow humans for hundreds of thousands of years.

Denial is a primitive and desperate unconscious method of coping with otherwise intolerable conflict, anxiety and emotional distress or pain. Psychiatrists are well aware of public denial and national denial as well as the ostrich concept which is figuratively burying one's head in the sand to deny a real problem.

Somehow the world is stuck on the idea that nations have supreme authority over themselves and that differences between nations can only be settled by war. If the world had invested the same amount of energy in trying to solve the problem of war as it invested in getting to outer space, it would have found the answer. The answer is limited world government.

The closest genetic relative to the human race is the chimpanzee, which shares our propensity to wage war but does not share our large brain. However, the chimpanzee has one huge advantage over the human race. That is the lack of intelligence to develop highly sophisticated and deadly weapons. The human race instead of using its brain to create a functioning world government to stop war, has used its large brain to engage in an arms race that has ended in a dead-end street instead of providing a solution to war.

Consider the following facts and make up your own mind if the human race is acting intelligently:

1. Humans have been violent to each other throughout its history and prehistory.

2. Humans share the tendency to wage war with its closest genetic relative, the chimpanzee.

3. Humans have no world government preventing war.

4. Humans have developed weapons of mass destruction which multiply the danger of the national control of events.

5. The United Nations honors the unilateral right of 193 nations to wage war at any time.

6. Humans also possess highly destructive weapons which are not weapons of mass destruction.

7. The United Nations has 5 countries that can stop any peace keeping action.

8. Humans live in a highly globalized world that did not exist when the United Nations was created.

When a person stands before a court for murder, the following excuses might be employed:

1. The person I killed made me mad in how he lives.
2. The person I killed does not share my religion.
3. The person I killed owned something I wanted.
4 The person I killed had a different economic system than I have and I was afraid he would convince others to be like him.
5. I am stronger than the person I killed.
6. I had a weapon and he did not.
7. My weapons are better than the ones he had.
8. I did not trust the person I killed.
9. He did not speak my language.
10. God told me to kill him.
11. I was afraid because he had weapons at home.

The list could go on, but no court would accept any of these excuses. Nations don't even have to give excuses. They are free to do whatever they want to do until they are forcefully stopped by some outside power. They should have no right to do whatever they want.

It seems reasonable to assume that because cultures condone killing other cultures without much thought, that this tendency to kill makes us more prone to kill others in our normal everyday lives. There is one thing for sure and that is the prohibition of killing in our everyday lives does not deter us from killing others in war.

The average person tends to assume that if a person is holding a position of political power, they are the most competent person for the job and were placed in that position because of that competence. In reality, political power has always been obtained by competing for the position of power. The desire to struggle for and exercise power has never been evenly distributed between persons. Some persons care nothing for doing that and some persons have an overwhelming need to do that. The early history of England had persons fighting over the opportunity to be the king. The vast majority of early English kings did not die a natural death.

A good example of the struggle for power in England in the early years is the Norman conquest of England by the Duke of Normandy, later called William the Conqueror. William had an arguable claim to the English crown through a distant relationship to the childless king Edward the Confessor. William came from France and defeated his rival Harold who died in the Battle of Hastings, and became king of England. These combatants who obviously had a high need to obtain and exercise power through any means (to the point of killing for it) were aided and abetted by their underlings who had little to gain.

Because the level of education is much greater today, the check on leadership power is greater in most circumstances. However, the same genes exist in the strivers for power today as existed in our violent past. Recorded history is one big study in violence and ignorance. We all have the genes of some murders in us because the murderers survived and procreated and the losers died and did not further procreate.

The human race prides itself on being highly intelligent because of having large brains. When we can send space ships into deep outer space, there seems a lot of justification for that opinion. However, the human race has laws against murder but has not figured out a way to prevent its 193 sovereign nations that comprise the United Nations from killing each other. When all it takes is a government to enforce murder laws between nations, continuing to do without such a government seems the most basic form of human ignorance.

Having 193 sovereign nations that can do anything they want and get away with it means the world's nations live in a lawless environment. You will not find any nation that will designate 193 of its people and tell them the law against murder does not apply to them. Soon you will have a lot less than 193 people that are not subject to the law of murder because many of the 193 will be dead. But the United Nations has created such an environment for the world's nations.

Psychologists have run an experiment where they designated certain persons to act like prison guards over other persons in the experiment. They set up the experiment without any enforceable rules for the "prison guards" to go by. The experiment had to be stopped before the conclusion of the experiment because there was so much violence and abuse against the "prisoners." This is the same environment that the "sovereign" nations of the United Nations live in.

Countries around the world define the killing of a human being in different categories depending on the culpability of the defendant's conduct. Distinctions are commonly made between unintentional killing and intentional killing. The severest punishments would commonly be reserved for intentional killing with premeditation. When a member of the United Nations starts a premeditated war, the combatants would have the mindset that merits the severest punishment under that country's laws. Since they are killing in war, the country does not punish them and actually rewards them with awards and recognitions.

Each nation in the world implicitly assumes when they go to war that they are on the defense and that their country is always right. Their military department is probably named a defense department and not an attack department. When they award a medal for brave performance in battle, they do not say that this was a war in which they were on the moral high ground. The reality is each participant in war is always considered by its country to be on the moral high ground. Even when a country is clearly attacked and, on the defense, that country is partially responsible for the attack by not supporting a world government to adjudicate disputes and prevent such attacks. When a country supports the present status quo, being attacked is in essence a self-inflicted wound. Each country of the world has clear moral responsibility for each war that happens.

The only countries that could complain about being attacked are those who have worked tirelessly trying to restructure the world to set up enforceable dispute resolutions between nations and the enforceable outlawing of murder by nations.

A thousand years ago the human race did not even know whether the earth was flat or round. Five hundred years ago it knew the world was round and was just beginning to understand that humans were spread all around the world. In the 17th century the human race invented the concept of national sovereignty after many human groups coalesced into nations. In the 20th century the United Nations was formed, technological developments increased greatly and globalization became a reality. At the present time, human interdependence has progressed to such an extent that a world government is clearly needed. The progression toward a world government will continue because it is the direction the world is moving. The issue for the world is if it is going to destroy itself in war before it saves itself from itself. Resistance to the direction the world is moving can have devastating consequences.

People make mistakes all the time. The biggest mistakes are not correcting your mistakes. It should be admitted that the present world structure does not solve the problem of war, and move on.

It is often difficult and risky to predict the future. However, one can say with absolute certainty that there will never be any peace in the world if any of the following occurs:

1. National sovereignty continues to be honored by the United Nations and or the international community.
2. The United Nations Security Council continues to have permanent members that can veto resolutions of the Security Council and amendments to the U.N. Charter.
3. The majority of the people of the world accept war as inevitable.
4. No world laws that are enforceable are in place to outlaw war between nations.
5. Nuclear weapons are not outlawed and destroyed.
6. Laws are not made and enforced to punish persons who kill in war.
7. There is no enforceable adjudication of disputes between nations.

Those who oppose a world government to prevent killing of fellow humans should project the probable trend of the development of the world into the future. The world population is not likely to decrease unless we have a nuclear holocaust or repeated pandemics. Destructiveness of military weapons is not likely to decrease. Globalization is likely to continue at a steady pace. Without a world government international anarchy will continue. Regional governmental entities such as the European Economic Union should increase in number and effectiveness. Global warming will get worse. Intercontinental ballistic missiles controlled by nations should proliferate. The United Nations should continue to ignore intra national wars as in Rwanda. The permanent members of the Security Council of the United Nations with veto powers should continue to block peacemaking.

The human race will continue to make war as it always has. Human beings will continue to die in war on a massive scale. Humans will continue to exhibit ethnocentrism. Humans will continue to exhibit xenophobia. National governments will continue to reward soldiers for being good murderers. Nations will continue to be imbued with the omnipotence of national sovereignty. Nations will still have no peaceful means of resolving disputes among themselves. International law will continue to be unenforceable.

Many philosophers will continue to believe that ethics does not apply to parties at war. The nations of the world will still have no explanation for why they punish murderers within their nation but do not do it in wars they are a party to. Powerful nations will continue to defeat weak nations because they want to. Good people will continue to look the other way and not stop killing in the world when there is a way to stop it. The United Nations will still be doing business in a world anarchy with only limited success in solving the problem of humans killing each other. The United Nations will still be doing business in a world anarchy which violates the universal declaration of human rights. The United Nations will still be advocating the rule of law when they operate without the rule of law in the world. Children would still be indoctrinated in loyalty to their nation instead of the world, making wars between nations all the more likely. There will still not be a world police force to enforce world law. The world would still be undecided whether killing another human being was bad or good.

People should not despair and feel like the world will never solve the problem of war which has gone on for hundreds of thousands of years. The human race has adjusted to new realities after being wrong forever. Humans adjusted themselves to the reality that tribes would not allow murders within the tribe. They adjusted themselves to the fact that cities would not allow killings within cities and later nations would not allow killings within nations. When Copernicus discovered that the sun did not revolve around the earth, people took it in stride. People did just fine when agriculture replaced hunting and gathering. We got over the idea that the best way to preserve historical information was by word of mouth. We did just fine when we discovered the earth was round and not flat. We adjusted to the new idea that making metal tools was better than stone tools. When we finally realized that the divine rights of kings were a myth, we survived.

War kills off our best men because the military eliminates the defective and unqualified before being admitted into the military service. Intelligence tests were invented during the first world war for the very purpose of selecting military personnel. Ostensibly, this is done because a country's survival is at stake. If a world government eliminated war, survival would not be at stake. A farmer or breeder of animals would never endanger their best stock; but this is exactly what the human race does.

Men have greater procreative potential than women because men can impregnate many women but a woman can usually only carry one child at a time. So, when our best men get killed in war, it has to have a long-range adverse effect on the human race because the men rejected from the military are free to sire the next generation.

Our ancient forebearers had a short life span and therefore fewer adults as a percentage of the population. If a population was primarily children and very young adults, the opportunity to be mature enough to reject violence as a solution to conflict essentially did not exist. Their traditions of violence to solve conflict have carried over until today when we should have the wisdom to find non-violent means of resolving conflict between nations. We are victims of our brainless violent heritage. Modern day underdeveloped countries have essentially the same problem that developed countries have had in their past. 1) few mature adults, 2) illiteracy, 3) poverty 4) habitual violence. The greatest gift that developed countries could and should give to the underdeveloped world is to stop by world law the violence between groups. This would allow the undeveloped world to concentrate on literacy and education instead of war. Plato in ancient Greece observed that people are like persons chained in a cave in darkness. He stated that those who have become enlightened should return to the cave and enlighten those ignorant of the truth. The educated world owes a moral obligation to stop the violence that seems so logical to unenlightened minds. No one except warlords benefit by others being ignorant of non-violent ways of living.

The invention of writing has changed the world. We now have a means for learning from our past in a manner other than word of mouth. The printing press, internet, and other means of communication have radically changed how the human race perceives their place in the world. If economist Adam Smith had published his book "The Wealth of Nations," that laid out the foundation principles for capitalism, two or more centuries prior to the date it was published March 9, 1776, it would have fallen on deaf ears. Capitalism essentially makes the consumer king, instead of conquering monarchs. Because consumers had become more educated and assertive by the time Adam Smith lived, capitalism had become an economic system that had wide appeal.

The rising assertiveness of persons through the printing press also is the reason modern democracies now exist. People demand to be in control of their own political future. However, under capitalism we get to choose the style of our clothes, but under democracies we don't get to be free from being killed in war. People in modern democracies need to demand that a limited world government puts an end to war, and it will take place.

There are many modern reasons for a world government. However, there is one reason that potentially could loom over all others. We now have the technology to edit genes in the human species as in other species. Can we rely on the social responsibility of selfish nations to properly control the editing of human genes? Individual nations should not have the power to control something that controls the destiny of the whole human species. A solution to this problem is imminent. We have had an arms race for thousands of years. Are we going to now have a race to which nation is going to be the first super race through gene editing?

It is a well-accepted economic fact that all nations profit by producing products that they can produce better and more economically, and then trading these products with other nations. The modern way of dealing with unpopular nations is through teaming up with allies and not trading with the unpopular nation or nations. This is called economic sanctions. The net effect of economic sanctions is that all the nations involved and in the world are damaged, not just the unpopular nations. This kind of self-destructive behavior would be unnecessary with a world government. The very idea of economic sanctions is an admission that the world is tightly interconnected economically, which has not always existed in the world's tradition of making war.

If we can affect other nations through economic sanctions, we can join together for peace in the whole world by demanding a world government to stop war.

The self-appointed policeman nations that try to affect errant nations through economic sanctions and war do not necessarily have the broad based confidence of other nations. We would not put up with self-appointed bullies in our communities. What the world lacks is a mechanism to have the world's people to express their desire for peace through an organization that outlaws war and stands behind that desire by virtual unanimity of the power forces in the world. Every functioning government distributes power such that the representation matches the power forces in the nation. We can do the same thing at the world level. Politicians are good at this. History shows that we know how to do it.

There is a real parallel between the belief in the divine right of kings and the present attitude that war makes logical sense. Kings who conquered their way into power easily convinced a largely illiterate public that they were divinely placed into power by God. That worked until the public became literate enough through the printing press to know better.

Nations now operate on the principle that war is inevitable because it has always been that way. When people become accustomed to the fact that the past does not match up with the present-day reality, they will not continue to cooperate with world anarchy that creates war.

Unless a business supplies war materials or is involved in the reconstruction of the damage caused by war, war is devastating for business. One of the first things a business person considers in making a new investment in a business is whether the country is at war or threatened by war. Successful businesses require a stable political environment. The present world anarchy has damaged business productivity and profit for too many generations to count. Peace would solve that problem going forward.

If you want to change human behavior for the better, war is not the way to do it. Behavioral psychologists know that punishment only shows one what not to do. It does not show what to do. Rewarding good behavior encourages good behavior and demonstrates right conduct. We comply without question with laws that have the backing of the populace, in most situations. We are used to laws passed in our nations that have a process for assuring that laws are passed with majority support. At the world level there is no such mechanism for determining majority support. We would rather fight wars with the hope of being the last nations in the conflict standing. The only argument in the favor of such an approach is that "we have always done it that way."

If we were attacked by another planet, we would see the logic of world government in a heartbeat. The reasons we can't see it is that we are trying to kill each other instead. That creates a perception of never being able to work together as a world. We can work together if we stop killing each other.

Chapter 9

"All nationalism can be understood as a kind of collective narcissism." – Geoff Mulgan

"Nationalism is power hunger tempered by self-deception." – George Orwell

Abraham Maslow gave the psychology profession his well-accepted idea that there is a hierarchy of needs that reads like this:

1) physiological needs such as food, water, oxygen, etc.
2) safety and security,
3) love and belonging,
4) self-esteem,
5) self-actualization.

Maslow said that when we have not satisfied the needs of a lower number indicated above, it is not possible to concern ourselves with the higher numbers.

Military units make sure their troops have physiological needs met, but have provided little or nothing listed with a higher number. The human race has never been able to have safety and security because of the ever-present threat of war. Nuclear non-proliferation is not nuclear elimination. It just preserves the military advantage of existing nuclear nations. There is one thing for sure and that is that a nuclear weapon will be used by a nuclear nation before being defeated in a war.

Countries are constantly watching their back even when no combat is taking place. This diverts our attention from reaching Maslow's higher needs. Consequently, the human race has always been psychologically stunted. We don't know what it means to be free of war and how much better off we would be without it.

Social psychology and cultural psychology study how social and cultural influences affect us mentally. Persons who support world anarchy and war should be asked to produce one such psychologist that says war is good for us mentally. That task is going to be hard to accomplish.

Persons who would argue that the world will never change its warlike ways which have been with us for as long as the human race has existed should consider the following:

Our larger brains have made us a supremely adaptable species. We have spread our species the world over and adapted to the new environments. In the process of this mobility and adaptability, we have created different cultures everywhere we went. Although a few animals have created the rudiments of cultures in isolated instances, we have created whole new cultures everywhere we have gone. Other animals are more limited in their behavior by instincts than we are.

In human cultures, children are indoctrinated in the culture in order to perpetuate it. By the time the children become adults, they are thoroughly trained in their culture. It is hard for an adult to start from scratch and retrain themselves in a new culture. This difficulty is among the several reasons why the human race is predisposed to fight and kill other cultures.

However, we don't live forever and succeeding generations have been the reason that the human race has spread the world over and adapted to new environments. The reluctance by adults to adapt to new cultures in the short run has created wars, but the human race has been very adaptable in the long run.

It's been said that the new generation never convinces the old generation of anything; the old generation just dies off. There is hope for the world in learning to not kill off each other in war.

Dogs are said to be man's best friend. We have been the ones who created the personality of dogs by selective breeding. We have created them just like ourselves. They wag their tail for friends and bark at outsiders. So do we.

Combining the xenophobic nature and implicit bias of the human race, with the fact that all nations seem to think war is the appropriate means to settle disputes, the present world situation is analogous to smoking in your dynamite factory.

Patriotism does just the opposite of what is needed for world peace. Patriotism explicitly creates an in-group/out-group feeling with the rest of the world. Patriotism expresses the short-term selfish interests of one nation and not the long-term interest of the nation and the rest of the world. We will never have world peace under the present conditions. We need to encourage our national citizens to look upon themselves as citizens of the world.

Behavioral psychologists understand that behavior can be modified by rewards as well as punishments. War attempts to modify behavior of any enemy through punishment. However, punishment has some downsides. It temporarily suppresses a response but does not weaken it. The punished response may reappear. Extremely strong punishment can cause abnormal behavior. Punishment does not tell you what to do, it only tells you what not to do.

War only delivers punishment; it does not tell a country

what to do. A World government is able to modify the behavior of countries through both rewards and punishments.

Psychologists know and have proven scientifically that the more familiar we are with something, the more favorable our attitude toward it. In the past, despots have capitalized on the general ignorance of the people to get the people to fight wars that largely benefited the despots. The ignorance of the people of other cultures made the people predisposed to fight other cultures. We live now in a vastly different world than in the past. Modern means of communication has made people more familiar with other cultures and, therefore, they have more favorable attitudes toward different cultures.

In the past, the relative ignorant were fighting the relatively ignorant. Today by and large, we have the relatively knowledgeable fighting the relatively knowledgeable. The reason we do this is that our political institutions have not caught up to the present reality. In the past, too much power was ceded to relatively local government. If we have become more familiar with other countries, we have less reason to fight them and we need to demand that the killing stops. In the future, the modern means of communication are only going to increase our knowledge of the rest of the world. We need to stop killing our neighbors.

When our existing governments were formed, no one knew that familiarity creates favorable attitudes. Science has only recently proven this.

Favorable attitudes are also created by physical proximity and psychological closeness. Psychologists have demonstrated this fact. Modern means of travel and population increases have given us greatly expanded proximity to our fellow humans. This in turn creates positive attitudes. This trend will only continue unless we destroy ourselves in nuclear war.

We have anarchy at the world level but in one sense we already have a defacto world government. The reason this is so is because all the nations of the world act as if they can make war whenever they don't like what another nation is doing; kill as many people as they want; and never be called to account for the killing. A government exists when the power forces in the community are in control and dictate what is to be done. This anarchical defacto world government will change when historical precedent ceases to require war and government is designed to fit present circumstances.

Bias toward out-groups does not have to be consciously realized. We as humans tend to particularize our feelings toward different members of our own in-group but not toward members of outgroups. In other words, our perception of members of outgroups is what is called outgroup homogeneity.

It plainly appears that a lot of our bias toward out-groups is not consciously realized. Anthony Greenwald and Mahzarin Benaji have developed an implicit associations test which measures fast or delayed response times when ingroup and outgroup information is matched with positive and negative words. This test reveals that persons have delayed response times on the test when outgroup information is paired with positive words. What they have found is that persons have implicit bias, though on a conscious level they think they have no bias.

Many research studies have been done since the work of Greenwald and Banaji on the subject of implicit bias. As if we had not perceived xenophobia in the human race in its long history, the work of Greenwald and Banaji prove objectively the human tendency to have problems dealing with persons who are not in our ingroup.

There is a good reason why the Diagnostic and Statistical Manual of the American Psychiatric Association does not list xenophobia in their list of mental disorders. Psychiatrists are in the business of diagnosing and treating mental disorders. There are several criteria for attempting to define abnormal behavior. A few of these are whether the behavior is maladaptive, whether it causes discomfort to the patient, whether it violates societies norms, and whether it is rarely seen. In the case of xenophobia, it doesn't seem to violate ingroup norms, it is pretty universal in the human race, it is maladaptive only at the outgroup level and is comfortable to the xenophobic person. Psychiatrists and psychologists cannot cure the whole world. The only way to be cure xenophobia is through education of everyone about everyone else. Ignorance is the hallmark of xenophobia. Dealing with xenophobia does not have a psychological solution, but it does have educational and political solutions.

We don't have to overtly teach our children that war is the accepted norm. Psychologists are well aware that people and particularly children learn by observation. All they have to do is watch the news media and see war taking place before their eyes. When this takes place without anyone discussing that it is ill-advised, learning talks place. War and preparing for war are such a large part of our lives, learning takes place without having to consciously instruct. When a world government outlaws war and peace prevails, we will be teaching peace and not war.

The fear of outsiders is in our DNA just like our fear of spiders and snakes. It developed from thousands of years of our ancestors having bad things happen with outsiders just like bad things happened with spiders and snakes. Our allowing war to continue teaches humans that bad things continue to happen with outsiders. If we had peace through world government, we would at least start to have natural selection make us more peaceful. Instead, we continue to have natural selection make us more warlike with the most destructive weapons of war that have ever existed in the world. We should make it harder for violent humans to live in a peaceful world. Their mal-adaptiveness will discourage their procreation.

The human race is not competent enough to be in possession of large destructive weapons such as nuclear weapons, chemical weapons, and other highly destructive weapons. There are many persons with personality disorders and mental disorders. Being in positions of power in order to engage these weapons is no guarantee of the mental stability and responsibility of these persons. Democracies make mistakes in whom they elect and autocracies by definition are controlled by persons with excessive needs to possess and exercise unnecessarily large amount of power.

A parent might allow their teenager to possess and use a BB gun. A parent should not allow their teenager to possess the large destructive weapons of today, because mass destruction is going to happen frequently. We have many individuals who never mature beyond the teenage level of decision making.

We all know that the history of war has been a male dominated activity. What may not be so obvious is that there is a good argument that war has not only been by men but for men.

To the extent that men have the potential to impregnate many women, they show themselves more interested in casual and promiscuous sex. Therefore, they have had an interest potentially in the whole small social group of primitive humans and have a stronger biological interest in protecting the whole small group. Women would be more interested in protecting the children they have raised, could raise or are raising. They are less interested in casual and promiscuous sex because of the need to be hands on involved in raising only a few children and usually only one at a time.

Women are thought by scientists to be attracted by males who have resources and social status. That would go a long way to explaining why men seem to strive for these things. The basic natures of men and women were formed over many thousands of years by natural selection in small groups.

What better way for a man to gain social status than being a successful warrior. Successful war leaders became the leaders of conquered territory. The examples of this are too numerous to bore the reader with. Every fighting male would like to be a war hero because we reward them, give them medals, etc. We reward them for killing outsiders, at the same time that we might severely punish them for killing within the group. Kings were successful warlords.

We are told by historians and anthropologists that practically all human cultures in the past were male dominated. Men fought the battles to gain control and they were not going to turn control over to women once control was obtained. The muscular and aggressive prowess of men would intimidate females into submission in the ingroup power structure as well. Why wouldn't men fight because they gained resources and status and sexual access just like wild animals do to this very day? The female preference for males with resources and status made them mate more with successful warriors, thereby creating continued generations of males inclined for more war.

What in the distant past was spinned as wars protecting the groups arguably was men gaining status for their benefit and for the sexual preferences of females. There is not much hope of voluntarily stopping war if we let females' sexual preference and male proclivity to war to continue unabated. If we had a female dominated history, we probably would have had few wars. Men should be praised for their actions in the past when war was often inevitable. They should be blamed now when it is not necessary. Men's nature more matched the needs of the past. Women's nature more matches the possibility for peace in the present and future. We should quit fighting wars just because it seems natural to men. We should stop wars because it makes sense even if men need to find something else to do to be fulfilled. The peacemaking skills of women is the wave of the future. The move of history in this direction is the reason for the rise in the status of women. Nine out of ten murders are by men. War fits the male genetically derived personality like a well-worn shoe.

Genetically, the human race has been skewed in the direction of aggression. Aggressive, pugnacious groups who won wars and created empires have spread their genes at the expense of the societies who lost wars and/or were killed by this process. This process of killing off those less adept at war is continuing to this very day. Unless war is outlawed, this process will continue to make the world more violent. You cannot fight wars for as long as the human race has done it without being genetically selected and adapted to war. The longer we continue to make war, the more we are inclined to do it.

The subject of war is not always dealt with in a conscious, rational manner. Humans psychologically try to avoid mental anxiety or the threat of mental anxiety. One way they deal with this is through unconscious defense mechanisms. War and the threat of war undoubtedly are anxiety producing and this anxiety can be relieved unconsciously.

If a person or nation has hostility toward another nation, the unconscious defense mechanism of projection can be employed to see in the other nation the hostility that actually exists in the person or nation that is doing the projection. "We dislike them" is converted into "they dislike us" through the unconscious use of projection. When the person or nation perceives the other nation as hostile, a vicious cycle of perceived hostility by both sides is created that did not previously exist. Nations that perceive hostility are more prone to act aggressively. When nations are hostile to one another, one or both nations may deny the problem and therefore ignore the problem. This has been called national denial. This can leave a nation in a vulnerable position that can lead to destruction. The problem of war will never be properly addressed by denying that a problem exists.

The threat of war can be buried from conscious consideration by the unconscious defense mechanism of repression. Just because one does not deal consciously with war through repression, does not mean it cannot affect the individual negatively from the unconscious mind.

Logical reasons for a world government to prevent war can be rationalized away by the defense mechanism of rationalization. The issue of war should be looked straight on and not ignored through rationalizations.

The excessive identification with one's nation prevents or discourages identification with the human race in general.

People can unconsciously employ affect dissociation where affect and emotional significance are separated from the subject of war to protect us from being upset by the actual horrors of war. This defense mechanism may make us feel better but it does not help with solving the problem of war.

The contradiction between the punishment for murders within nations and the encouragement and acquiescence to homicide between nations in war creates a mentally disturbing issue for the mind to process. We go about our lives everyday by not thinking about this contradiction by using the unconscious defense mechanism of compartmentalization. Thus, we engage in the process of emotional segregation of these two emotionally charged contradictory subjects. Following the established traditions of war is any easy way to avoid trying to cure the problem of killing in war.

One of the reasons we are stuck in the tradition of making war is the fact that our world has never changed so rapidly as it has in the last two hundred years and we do not know how to deal with it. In the distant past we lived in a world that, by modern standards, changed very slowly. Because of that there was a premium on teachability and absorbing and conforming to inherited wisdom. Today, because of democracy and capitalism, entrepreneurs try to outdo each other to appeal to consumers and innovation has mushroomed. We are ill prepared to deal with rapid change because even though we have large brains we are genetically predisposed more to learn from the past than to adjust to a rapidly changing world.

It's not only adults who discriminate against outgroups. Children at about 8 months of age develop stranger anxiety which expresses itself in extreme expressions of fear of strangers. This happens at about the time when children become mobile and protects the children and the ingroup from possible dangers from unknown persons. It is reasonable to conclude that this fear carries over to our treating outgroups different from our ingroups. Xenophobia would be then an extreme form of this common human characteristic. When our children show signs of stranger anxiety, we respond with understanding and consoling behavior. When adults have stranger anxiety, we give them a weapon and send them to war.

Stranger anxiety in children would not be cultural but applicable to children in general. It would have developed in the tens of thousands of years when humans were few and children would only be familiar with those in their own small group. Strangers would be those in other groups or on the margins of the small ingroups. What develops in the child matches up well with those humans who have fought in war in the past. We are genetically adapted to a world that no longer exists.

It would appear that our tendency to kill our fellow humans in war is not really to protect our genes as has been assumed in the past. We are told that our genes are 99.9% similar to other humans. We used to not even know what a gene was, much less how similar we are to other humans.

It is certainly true that our cultures vary from each other over the world by more than .1%. It's a matter of fighting different cultures instead of fighting other genes. No parent is 100% biologically the same as their child and we certainly aren't predisposed to kill our children. We are so closely related to other people genetically; we should be kinder to them.

To clarify the need for a world government to stop war, the reader should pose a question to a person who knee jerks a response that opposes such a solution. Ask them their reasons for their opposition. The list of reasons given should be very short and will not be substantial reasons. The unspoken reason will be that it will require such a large change in how the world functions now. The person should be ready to explain why a person in one country who lives a tenth of a mile away from the next country could join the military in his country and kill any number soldiers in the neighboring country with impunity; and be prosecuted for murder for killing his neighbor a tenth of a mile away is his own country. Ask for the reasons for the different treatment.

Persons in countries with adequately functioning governments have a sense that their lives are under a just system. There are leaders making decisions primarily for the good of the community. They drive on the side of the road that is prescribed by law and they don't resent this type of direction. At the international level, this sense of a just society does not exist. The international community functions like a "family" that has no parent. Nations internally have means of taking the interests of different persons and groups into consideration in making decisions. At the international level this does not exist. Every nation has its own self-interest but there is no means of compromising and moderating these interests and making decisions with input from everyone. The result is war.

War rides on the back of fear of other cultures. The internet and global communication have changed everything. Behavioral psychologists cure phobias by gradually approaching the feared situation. The internet and global communication have done this for us and the effects of these will be even greater in the future. The World Bank and similar organizations should concentrate on putting the internet in the hands of every human being, providing for online translation services and supporting literacy. When this happens, the lack of fear of other cultures will erase the depersonalization of unknown persons and war should decrease. Not having to be constantly prepared for war would be the greatest economic advantage any poor country could hope for. Continuation of war is reinforcing the natural tendency toward fear of other cultures. This fear was developed in our genes because bad things happened in our interactions with other cultures. By continuation of war, we are making sure that bad things continue to happen. This has just the opposite effect of curing phobias through benign exposure to what is feared.

In the past, the human species was too diverse to effectively even attempt a world government to stop war. That was then and this is now. Today we have the means to become somewhat familiar with all cultures. That was not true in the past.

We have evolved in our thinking about the appropriateness of fighting duels when we have a disagreement with someone. Today, fighting a duel would be prosecuted as aggravated assault or murder, and we would not look the other way. However, we still think countries fighting a war is just the way you do things. We need to evolve in our own thinking about war just as we have evolved in our thinking about duels. It makes no sense to punish a duelist and not punish a national warrior. Having a disagreement with someone does not justify killing them whether it involves individuals or countries.

War in the distant past took place in a world where few humans existed and therefore there was less chance of war. Today we have a greater chance of war because of our increased population. Also, the rising world temperatures increase the chances for war because more aggression takes place in high temperatures.

In many species, the males fight with each other, but they usually do not kill each other. Humans are not smart enough to refrain from killing each other. We pride ourselves in being smart but we are very selective in what we use as examples to prove this.

Social learning theorists have demonstrated how aggression can be learned and how this can affect later generations. This also applies to chimpanzees, which are our closest relatives. However, chimpanzees are not smart enough to know this. We are smart enough to know this, but continue to teach aggression to our progeny. Before the science of psychology existed, we did not know this; but now we have no excuse for passing learned aggressive behavior on to posterity.

The veto power in the United Nations of the victors of the 2nd world war and their nuclear weapons capability creates a situation where these nations can bully other countries with impunity. Any nuclear weapon country is effectively immune from defeat in war against non-nuclear weapon countries. The reason is that their nuclear weapons will always be deployed before being destroyed by a non-nuclear weapon country. This is the reason why the United Nations has been ineffective in stopping wars between non-nuclear weapon countries. The psychological defense of displacement is taking place. It operates like what happens when your boss does something you don't like which you can't do anything about; but you go home and kick your cat.

Within nations we do not allow killing as a means to settle private disputes between persons and groups. However, at the international level, all nations acquiesce in war as a means to settle disputes between nations. There are practical reasons why that will be difficult to change. Despotic national leaders acquired their power through force or the threat of force, and see no reason for any change in that system. Democratic national leaders are afraid of being defeated in elections if they do not represent their constituencies on the world arena, by protecting their voters by using or threatening force as is allowable under the present international anarchy. The only way we will ever have world peace is if the people demand it.

In a world government each nation would still be able to assert their parochial interests but the countries not in a dispute would have the balance of power in determining the outcome in a dispute.

The means to learning about other cultures is so easily available today, we should not structure our political institutions to cater to the willfully ignorant. Learning what other cultures have to offer to us is a moral responsibility. Ignorance historically was understandable. Today, it is not! The better customs around the world are available to be stolen for our own use. Our worst customs compared to other customs can be freely abandoned.

Xenophobia in itself may not initiate a war, but it sure makes for willing participants in a war started for other reasons. Take away xenophobia and war is greatly diminished. Trying to cure xenophobia is like trying to cure the whole human race. The way to reduce xenophobia is through education and reducing ignorance. It is a known fact that persons from areas with less exposure to other cultures are more xenophobic.

War polarizes people in different countries, which exacerbates lack of learning about other countries, which exacerbates xenophobia, which exacerbates war. War causes war.

Peace encourages social interaction, which creates gaining knowledge of other countries, which reduces xenophobia, which creates a continuation of peace.

Peace creates peace. On the subject of war, the human race is a victim of the large brains that we have. There may be very basic culture in a few species, but creating cultures is a human phenomenon. When we create cultures that are unique to our groups, we are requiring our children to acquire complex unique methods of living. This can take a lifetime or at least a substantial portion of a lifetime. When different cultures interact, their members are forced with having to start all over again if they are controlled by a new culture. This prospect creates fear and xenophobia. Our big brains made it possible for humans to essentially inhabit the whole world except Antarctica. This furthered the tendency of cultures to vary from one another. It is said you can't teach an old dog new tricks. Expecting humans to act unemotionally about the prospect of a reculturization is unrealistic.

We can't change our large brains or the tendency to create cultures or the lack of adaptability to start all over when we age. We can encourage and not discourage cultural exchange and communication the world over. We can create a world government to stop war. It is proven that children are more adaptable than adults and acculturation to the world should start with children. Our xenophobia and war developed over the tens of thousands of years when humans had essentially no means to learn about other cultures. Today we don't have that as an excuse. Our increased life space allows us to learn at least partially about all cultures.

When a species through natural selection develops more adaptable ways of living, the adaptation can have some unadaptable side effects. In the case of humans, our large brains have given us an advantage despite that we have made war with our own species, invented self-destructive devastating weapons and become xenophobic. With war we have dug ourselves a hole. We need to use our large brains to get us out of our hole.

Psychologists and historians demonstrate that humans are affected by their tendency to conform to others about most anything and to follow the dictates of authority. Both of these tendencies make war more likely when war is the acceptable means of settling disputes.

We are so different than our past we are like adults who have grown up from our past. People change and cultures change. We should be ashamed of ourselves for brainlessly following our warlike history and act no differently than our history. We are better than that. We teach our children the past of war, but not what is possible in the future.

Bernard MT Condensed and Minion Pro on LSI archival white
Type and Design by Karen Paul Stone

www.ingramcontent.com/pod-product-compliance
Lightning Source LLC
Chambersburg PA
CBHW031812190326
41518CB00006B/301

9781947589520